Divergent EDU:

*Challenging assumptions and limitations to create
a culture of innovation*

Mandy Froehlich

Divergent EDU
Mandy Froehlich

Published by EduMatch®
PO Box 150324, Alexandria, VA 22315
www.edumatch.org

Dedication

To Dan, Brycen, Goose, Cortlynne, Addisyn, my
family and friends, #my53s and the rest of my
professional learning family, to my mentor and
friend George Couros, and to Sarah Thomas
whose faith in me is unconditional and
unwavering:
Thank you.

Table of Contents

Preface

I have often wondered what makes some people successful at an endeavor and others not. Why is it that some teachers in the same school will create relationships with students and push innovative boundaries in teaching and others will forget students' names and wheel out their overhead projector every day? What is the difference between one teacher being successful without an abundance of support and another teacher won't move forward without pushing, prodding, and constant reassurance?

The reason that education can be difficult (and also so rewarding) is the variety of personalities, perseverance, background stories, and experiences, among a million other differences we all bring to the table. Where we sometimes get it wrong is expecting that everyone will react the same to certain circumstances, when in reality "fair isn't always equal" applies to adults as well. We have teachers with mental health issues, both known and unknown disabilities, ones who have suffered trauma, and those who have lived through personal and professional adversity. While we need to be sensitive to everyone's needs when we plan or implement anything, the strengths and differences we have are also what make us a stronger unit. When we begin to look at the people we work with through the lens of everyone is doing the best job they can with what they have, you begin to see the opportunities for support instead of their only their weaknesses. An us versus them attitude will get us nowhere. I often use "we" throughout the book to refer to a group of people as being "all of us." Administrators were once teachers, and divergent thought is not specific to one role. There is no blame, only acceptance of our own strengths and weaknesses and subsequently, growth.

This book will provide information on common issues that I've experienced in education and how we may either become more aware or address them outright. But, the focus throughout will be on the overarching question from the book: how can we all support one another to be the educators we want to be for both our students and ourselves?

Foreword

By George Couros

I met Mandy Froehlich several years ago at a conference in Minnesota and was blown away by two characteristics that she embodied in meeting her personally: her curiosity and desire to grow and learn combined with a drive to serve others to bring out their best. As I read through her book, I was so pleased to find that both of these qualities jumped off the pages to push thinking while also encouraging people to find their own solutions in their own context. I am a big believer in the idea that there is no carbon-copy solution that will work for students in any context. But when educators ask questions and find their own solutions to serving the students in front of them, this is when schools truly become innovative and forward-thinking. Innovation and divergent thinking are not about doing what the school or the classroom across the way is doing and trying to keep up, they are about finding your own solutions to improve learning opportunities for those you serve, both the adults and the students.

When we think of "innovation" we often think of things like YouTube, the iPhone, and the Slap Chop (the greatest food dicing product in my lifetime). In reality, we should be thinking about the people and situations that provided the opportunities for those things to be created. At the heart of innovation is people, and throughout the book, Mandy finds the balance of pushing ideas while still honoring the personal needs of educators to grow as not only teachers but more importantly, as people.

As you read this book, I encourage you to ask, "how does this apply to our context?" and write or share a solution. Reflection is crucial to moving forward, but moving forward is also crucial to moving forward. Use this book as a guide to push thinking and provide some ideas on how you can improve opportunities for those you serve — but don't just consume, create. Figure out a way, find a way, and then lead the way.

Mandy will push your thinking, but for true growth to happen, take the opportunity to learn from her suggestions. Then create your own pathway for yourself, and find ways to be the pathway for others. I have seen Mandy do this exact thing with so many educators who feel so empowered after their time with her, and I know this book can do the same for you if you are open to it.

Happy reading!

Chapter 1

The Brick by Brick
Building of the Hierarchy

Divergent Teaching

"Becoming Fearless isn't the point. That's impossible. It's learning how to control your fear, and how to be free from it, that's the point."
-Divergent, Veronica Roth

I remember reading and devouring the young adult novel Divergent by Veronica Roth a few years ago when the book had first been released, and I was fascinated by the play on the quality of being divergent. Basically, in the book, being divergent was a characteristic that was to be hidden, hunted, and eradicated. The act of thinking divergently was considered dangerous, deviant, and played outside of that society's norms. Why? Because individuals displaying that behavior didn't conform to what was expected. They questioned everything, had new ideas, and thought outside the fences that society had created. While in the book having divergence was something to be ashamed of and feared, in my mind, thinking divergently and being labeled as divergent would be considered a high honor.

Although the dictionary definition of divergent is fairly simple, moving or extending in different directions from a common point, the psychological definition of divergent is: *(of thought) using a variety of premises, especially unfamiliar premises, as bases for inference, and avoiding common limiting assumptions in making deductions* (Merriam Webster, n.d.). There are few definitions that define more closely what we should be doing in education. In all areas, our own professional learning, our work with children, we should be challenging our own assumptions, and looking for ways to meet our own learning needs and the needs of kids both educationally and emotionally. We should be self-checking our own limitations in our thinking. Finding ways to expand our knowledge base. Analyzing areas where we may be *wrong*. Therefore, the definition I've developed for divergent teaching is:

The ability to recognize our own assumptions, look for limitations, and challenge our own thinking in regard to teaching and learning. It's taking an idea and creating new thinking that will facilitate student learning in new, innovative directions for deeper understanding. It is diverging from the norm, challenging current ideas, looking for a variety of solutions, and a willingness to learn from failure and grow.

Educators who embrace divergence when making decisions will ensure they are taking in all the possible angles and solutions, including the ones that they are not as familiar with or especially ones that make them uncomfortable. They will avoid allowing assumptions and unknowns to limit their thinking all the time, but especially in making decisions. In order to make this work, they need to be more reflective as they look for areas where they might be blinded and places where they might be assuming. They will need to become more comfortable with being uncomfortable, and relentless in the pursuit of learning what is unfamiliar. The educator will recognize and control their fears in the steps and decisions needed to reach goals. By following this way of thinking, divergence will allow them to become better, more informed decision-makers and more comfortable in implementing innovative leadership or teaching strategies.

Divergent Educators

In a collaborative blog post with friend and author of *Take the L.E.A.P., Ignite a Culture of Innovation* (2019), Elisabeth Bostwick and I developed what we feel are the qualities of a divergent teacher. Divergent teachers have certain characteristics that differentiate them from others. While the definition requires them to challenge current ideas and their own assumptions, there are additional qualities that are ingrained in their divergence. The combination of these attributes results in a well-rounded, innovative and divergent thinker.

Deeply reflective

Divergent teachers recognize that significant growth cannot happen without taking time for deep reflection. They know how they reflect best, whether it's through writing, meditating, or driving quietly in their car on the way home. They have strategies in place to allow them to take the time and hold reflection in high regard as one of the reasons they are who they are professionally. Deep reflection goes beyond what could go differently in a recent lesson. It also leads an educator down the path of discovering how their own beliefs and assumptions affect what they do in the classroom or how they perceive and communicate with others. Understanding the difference between surface-level reflection and deep reflection is an integral part of divergent thought. Once you understand what you believe, how it affects what you do and how you are perceived, it is easier to change your behavior and push yourself forward.

Courageous

Divergent teachers understand the importance of taking thoughtful risks. However, just because they understand the unmatched learning that can occur when risks are taken doesn't mean that they don't fear taking risks. They may still feel anxiety (especially if they work in a compliance-based culture) but they are courageous enough to move forward anyway because they understand the reward outweighs the risk. This characteristic often has the potential to spark courage in others too. When we, as educators, are transparent and demonstrate the risks we're taking, along with our vulnerabilities, we inspire others to join hands with us, collaboratively creating enhanced learning experiences for our youth.

Tenacious

Tenacity is a hallmark of anyone who assumes risk and is passionate about moving forward. To fail and repeatedly get back up and try again takes the kind of tenacity that requires a significant amount of strength, reflection, and personal growth to achieve. Sometimes failing can be difficult especially if what we tried is particularly far out of our comfort zone or something we really wanted to go right. This trait of a divergent teacher keeps them moving forward when others might quit.

Voracious learner

At all stages of our journey, we embrace learning as an ongoing process. There is no finality, but instead continuous growth. Divergent teachers learn in multiple ways; through reading, reflective writing, peer observations, collaborative conversations, seeking meaningful feedback, and considering how they can improve through goal setting. They are cognizant to learn from their mistakes and retool to move toward growth. With the understanding that transformation doesn't happen overnight, they frequently immerse themselves in opportunities that foster deep

learning and then employ new findings to the
classroom. In doing so, they identify what works
best for their learners and share with colleagues to
contribute to the culture of learning.

Mentor

Divergent teachers have a sincere
appreciation for uplifting and adding value to
others to elevate education. They grasp that it's
essential to inspire collective efficacy, producing a
positive, long-lasting impact on learner
achievement. In addition to providing support
through developing trusting relationships, they
demonstrate help-seeking as well, contributing to
the understanding that each individual has
strengths to contribute. Collaboration is often
referenced as a necessary component of effective
teaching and it is. However, collaboration should
be the baseline expectation. Mentorship brings an
additional quality to collaboration that focuses on
not only the give-and-take but also the guidance,
support, and high expectations that only a mentor
can provide.

Thinking divergently is a quality I'd like to
nurture and cultivate for myself and the people
around me, but similar to the Divergent series, it is
something that isn't necessarily revered, even in our
education society. I have gotten "the look" many
times when I've come up with a new idea that I've
wanted to implement. As an administrator, it's the
look of questioning how my idea is going to affect
everyone else. As a teacher, it was the look from
other educators of *"how am I supposed to keep up*

with her and all her ideas (i.e. Is she going to make me look bad by trying something awesome)?" While the idea of divergence is hypothetically something that many people would embrace, the practice of it can make people feel uncomfortable enough to ignore or outright detest it.

Innovation

Innovation has definitely become one of society's major buzzwords. It doesn't matter whether you're looking at the public or private sector, everyone is trying to be more innovative. Unfortunately, not many people take the time to actually define innovation, and because education is its very own beast, time is rarely taken to define innovation as it relates to educators and students. The best definition I've found for innovation is from George Couros's Innovator's Mindset (2015) where he defines innovation as an idea, concept, or product that is new, different, and better. It doesn't have to be something completely new, but can also be a new way to use the original idea.

Couros goes on to say that innovation is a personal journey. This is powerful because if you view innovation as a thing, you're not sure if you can achieve it. But, if you view innovation as a journey, you feel like you can take your own path to get there. The latter is very true. As Couros explains, what is innovative to one might not be innovative to another if they have been doing it already. For example, in my technology integrator role, I helped some teachers learn about and implement design thinking. However, there are still some people who are just discovering this innovative way of learning and that is okay. The teachers that worked with me are a little further on their journey than others might be, and there are people who are further along on theirs than I am. The most important thing to remember is that everyone has to start somewhere. I am a Google Trainer now and can navigate Google fairly well, but there was once a day long ago when I had never heard of Google Slides, and I guarantee there is a trainer who knows it better than I do.

This same concept can also be seen in technology and how it is ever changing at a rapid pace. I remember the pure elation when I was finally able to get my green LG Slider Phone after some weeks of admiring others' from afar. There was an actual keyboard and there was no more pressing 2 to get to A, only to press it one too many times and get to B, and then need to keep going around until you got back to A...being careful not to hit it too many times, hoping you're not being too slow that it moves onto the next letter space. Now, no doubt, there would be either snickers or looks of pity from the updated virtual keyboard users if I ever pulled the LG out. The only way our kids have ever seen something like this was if we kept it in order for them to use as a play phone.

Another example: interactive boards. Years ago, the first district I was ever in had one SMART board in the computer lab of the middle school. Only teachers were allowed to touch it, and I didn't dare even do that. I was so afraid of getting fingerprints on it. Students, should they earn the privilege of touching it, had to go to the restroom and clean their hands with soap first, or at a bare minimum get a hand check for cleanliness. However, a few weeks ago I had a discussion with my device manager about how we were going to find a dumpster large enough to get rid of our interactive boards in favor of interactive panels. I've said this in districts that don't have interactive boards in all the classrooms and have heard the audible gasps. I've also said that in districts who have interactive panels and seen their nods of approval. Districts, too, are all on their own journeys of innovation.

Can't make a personal connection with the phone or interactive boards examples? Well, even the technology that takes care of our most basic needs is changing. Currently, I have very basic water-efficient toilets in my house. But the newest, most innovative toilets, pricing at around ten thousand dollars apiece, have functions that make going to the toilet an experience. It automatically detects someone approaching and lifts the lid, gets the seat ready for you by heating it up, and has an aerated "cleanse" as well as a dryer, of course. Don't like cleaning the toilet? It has a bacteria-killing UV light cleaner that will eliminate the toilet brush industry. Now, while these are new and seem full of unusual, unnecessary features, this is definitely something that 15 years from now has the potential for being inexpensive enough for people to afford. It may be in most homes because that is typically how new innovation works. We want it but it's expensive, it gets cheaper, we buy it, it becomes the norm, we look toward the new and different. Even long ago the Greek Philosopher, Heraclitus, knew "Life is Flux"-Panta Rhei in Greek, meaning everything or all things change (Mark, 2010).

So, how is innovation and divergent thinking linked? Thinking divergently will lead to innovative change, ideas, and growth. As we, as educators, challenge our own assumptions and thinking, we are more likely to think in ways we haven't before, which can lead to innovation whether it's in our lessons, our ideas, or a product. Many times, it's the limitations we place on ourselves that hamper our growth. In challenging that, we will be more likely to move forward.

Teacher Support for Divergence and Innovation

When I was an elementary teacher, our district went 1:1 with iPads. At the time, we didn't focus professional learning on technology, nor did we have any kind of embedded support. One of the district techs wheeled the cart into my classroom and gave me the equivalent of a "good luck." Prior to the start of the school year, we had a 20-minute training on how students would log in to their iPads. This type of rollout implementation wasn't unusual at the time in many districts. The innovation was considered the distribution of the devices and less of an emphasis was placed on how the devices supported learning in innovative ways.

I was lucky because my passion was technology, and so it was in my interest area to try to find ways for students to create with the technology that we had. I began using the iPads to document student learning in e-portfolios and largely focused on student content creation, which back then was definitely diverging from the norm. But for other teachers who didn't have the same passion for tech, they struggled with the use of the iPads in the classroom. They would be used for lower-level Google searches and a way to do math facts and worksheets online, not yet realizing that a worksheet online is still just a worksheet. While I would consider these activities a normal place to start a journey, without district-supported learning or embedded coaching, the teachers never began their innovative journey beyond substituting encyclopedias and worksheets. They didn't have the interest or support to do so.

My interest in educational technology and the fact that I became burnt out in the classroom led me to take a technology integrator role in a neighboring district. I was excited at this prospect because the job encompassed exactly what I felt was missing as a classroom teacher, and as they had hired nine technology integrators for the first time, I looked forward to being a part of a team that was developing the role.

My main goal when I started was to build capacity and change attitudes. As a group, we often joked about building capacity to the point that we would work our way out of our jobs. But I consistently found myself fixing technology and occasionally showing a teacher an edtech tool when I found the time. It became almost a game in which I would go to a classroom and find the offending technology, plug in a cord, turn it off and then turn it back on, and then corner the teacher and ask about their curriculum in hopes they would invite me into their classroom. Even with my best attempt at puppy-dog eyes, the enthusiasm for my support was minimal. In no way was I meeting my personal-professional goal. Because I looked at technology through the lens of someone who was passionate about it, I couldn't imagine why teachers would very nearly break out in a run the other way when they saw me coming. To me, this was exactly what I had been looking for as a teacher: the support of someone who knew just a little more in an area where I wanted to grow. What I didn't understand at the time was that it had really had nothing to do with what *I wanted* in the past as a teacher or currently as the technology integrator. It was about what *the teachers needed*, and they were not ready for me yet because they had so many other issues that were stealing their focus. They didn't have the headspace to even think about being innovative, let alone necessitate learning something new, especially if technology was not one of their passions.

One step that I took to try to remedy this issue was to create what I called **Innovation Teams**, which will be discussed in detail in an upcoming chapter. In short, Innovation Teams were teams of teachers across three schools who voluntarily gave up their time to study innovative teaching strategies and develop their divergent thinking. When my views on innovation began to shift from being almost completely based on technology to residing more in learning, I needed to find a more concrete way to provide teachers with the support they needed. That's when the idea of Innovation Teams was born. I worked and muddled through this new team, made mistakes, but also saw amazing buy-in, growth, and enthusiasm for teaching where it might have been diminished before. I actually had a teacher say to me, "I was starting to question why I was teaching anymore, but I've found such a renewed sense of why I went into teaching in the first place. I am so excited to implement these ideas as soon as possible!" At that point, I knew I was taking the right steps in providing teachers who had gotten lost along the way with the support they needed to be the awesome leaders and learners I already knew they were.

However, my attention was drawn to an interesting problem that I encountered throughout the process with the Innovation Teams: I had teachers who had complete buy-in to the idea, but still struggled with implementation because of outside forces that had nothing to do with being innovative or divergent. Instead, it was adversity that was connected with other issues like climate and culture, mindset, and leadership. Time of course, was always a factor, especially considering their professional learning was dictated by the district and they weren't given the autonomy to dive into what they really desired to learn. I also found it interesting that the type and magnitude of issues that were present varied across buildings. In one building, it was the perceived lack of support from the leadership that was causing a bump in their path, while in another building it was the overall mindset teachers had toward their own abilities, even though their new leadership was strong and supportive. And if these teachers who were excited about innovation, had a propensity for divergent thinking, and had buy-in to the process were struggling, what did that mean for our teachers who hadn't reached even those levels yet?

Developing the Hierarchy

I began by trying to delineate what needed to be in place for an educator to really have the best chance of being innovative in their roles and develop their divergent teaching skills. Asking myself, "how do I make people more innovative?" was not only a daunting question, *but the wrong one*. I knew I could not force people to be more innovative. In fact, fostering any kind of change in thinking takes time and support. Compliance measures will most likely have the opposite effect. This would especially be the case with divergent thinking where the premise is challenging one's own thoughts and assumptions.

When I started reflecting and considering what was really deterring the teachers' forward movement in their innovation journey, many of the barriers actually had very little to do with innovation or technology. These teachers, through the process of the Innovation Teams, knew that innovation had more to do with a way of thinking than a device. It was not the type or lack of devices stopping them. It was the distraction of the barriers that was taking away from their ability to be the divergent teachers they wanted to be. What was missing were the pieces of the educational ecosystem that supported creativity, innovation, and divergent thinking. How we could best serve educators could be to create an atmosphere where they have everything they need in place to be innovative and in turn, give their students a chance to be innovative as well.

The experiences within my own district and others in which I consulted led me to believe that certain common issues would take away from the opportunity for teachers to dive into divergent teaching strategies: climate and culture, leadership, mindset, and professional development. A disruption in any of these areas would detract from the educator's headspace; how full our brains are at any given moment!

For example, if I'm working in a toxic climate, I may be walking down the hall and hear several other teachers complaining about students- which bothers me. Later, I sit and think about how I wish those teachers wouldn't do that, regret that I didn't stop and say something, and plan what I'm going to say the next time. I may allow it to bother me for most of the day and night, maybe complaining to my spouse, depending on the severity of what they were saying. All of these thoughts take up headspace. They take up time. They steal energy. Every thought I had about those teachers was headspace, time, and energy that I could have been using toward diverging from my normal teaching routine and being innovative.

I want to be clear that this is not a psychological or medical term (that I know of). This is how I describe the way my own brain works. Simply, it has space. I choose what uses that space and gains my attention.

The Hierarchy of Needs for Innovation and Divergent Thinking was born from the idea that we need to provide support to teachers, so they have the chance to be more innovative and divergent thinkers. There are four foundational levels with three focus areas each that support the peak of innovation and divergent thinking: climate/culture, effective leadership, mindset, and professional learning. The hierarchy levels are each of the areas that I've found that might possibly distract educators from their own growth. The hierarchical structure is not to say that one of them needs to be complete before the others can develop, nor are they gamified levels, but rather they are foundational levels that provide support to each level above them. It's not that a level is going to be completely missing in a district. Similar to Maslow's Hierarchy of Needs, there are holes in each level that need to be filled. Some schools, or even people, are closer to having strong foundations in all areas than others. All districts have their issues, but the effectiveness and strength (or lack thereof) of their foundations can have varying effects on the quantity and quality of teacher support.

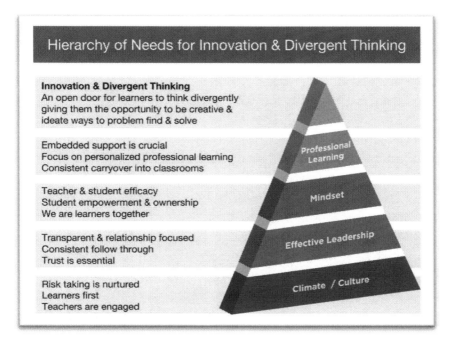

The placement of each level is not haphazard. There are reasons for each of the locations. I also discovered that the higher you go in the hierarchy, the more the change moves from an organizational focus to an individual change. For example, a change in climate and culture is more of an organizational change than personalized professional learning which is really about what an individual needs and pairing that with support. That means that as you move up the hierarchy, the individual support needed to create change increases because the changes that need to occur become changes that needs to happen *within people* versus at an organizational level.

For example, Bill works in a school that has worked diligently to fill the holes in their climate and culture issues. Their leadership has changed over, and the new principal is very supportive of teachers, transparent, and values personalized professional learning. There is organizational support on mindset. The school has studied Carol Dweck's work on growth mindset and there is buy-in among the teachers in general. They have adopted the growth mindset common language, and the staff as a whole has begun to shift their beliefs. The organization (school) has provided Bill with everything it can to learn about growth mindset and adopt that same thinking. However, Bill has not, and in order to fill the holes in mindset, he will have a more difficult time tackling personalized professional learning when he needs to believe that he has the ability to learn and grow. The school gave him the opportunity and support to fill the holes in mindset, but he needed to make the choice to change his thinking. That is where the hierarchy begins to get more individualized. The organization can provide support, but the final change needs to happen within the individual.

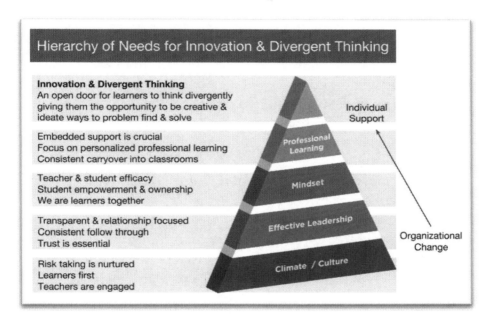

Placement of the Foundational Levels

As previously stated, the foundations have specific placements due to what I felt needed to be in place to support the levels above. Like a house that has already been built, all of these pieces are already present in every district. Every district, school, and classroom has a climate and culture. Every district, school, and classroom has a mindset. The question is whether the climate and culture (or the mindset) established within these ecosystems allows for the educators working in that system to be supported how they need to be. If not, there are holes in that foundation that need to be addressed and filled to provide the most structurally sound foundation as possible. And the first step in this process is of course, being honest, reflective, and truly recognizing where holes might exist in order to fill them. One cannot fix a problem that they're not willing to address. Briefly, the reasoning for the placement levels is as such, but will be addressed in greater detail in their corresponding chapters.

In workshops, I've asked people to build their own hierarchies, and many times they begin with effective leadership. I absolutely will not disagree that an effective leader will cultivate a successful team, but put an ineffective leader on that same team and it may become dysfunctional. While I agree that this argument demonstrates the critical importance of effective leadership, I believe that climate and culture are the foundation of everything we do. I also believe that if you place an effective leader in a negative climate and a weak culture, they will spend all their time trying to right the ship. They won't have the energy to support their teachers as best as they could as if they walked into a building with a positive climate and strong culture. Therefore, climate and culture became the foundation of the hierarchy.

This foundation of leaders includes administration as one might typically imagine, but it also includes teacher leaders, student leaders, community leaders, and parent leaders. This leadership will drive the foundational level of mindset by providing opportunities for learning and support around growth and innovator's mindsets and create the buy-in needed for developing divergent thought and innovative teaching strategies.

Once a culture that encourages and supports a growth and innovator's mindset has been established and educators believe that their own abilities are not fixed, they will be able to effectively participate in true personalized professional learning where they have ownership of their professional goals with support from leadership. If a culture valuing these characteristics is not in place, educators will perceive any attempt at goal-setting as another compliance initiative and may only put forth as much effort as one would expect into something where you feel no connection. Therefore, mindset supports the foundational level of professional learning.

Finally, all professional learning- especially personalized professional learning, gives an educator the background knowledge and growth that they need to be innovative and divergent thinkers. All of the preceding foundational levels support the apex of the hierarchy, which is the open door for educators to think divergently and innovatively. Again, with the focus swinging toward more individualized choices as you move up the foundational levels, the onus still remains with the educator to take the innovative and divergent risks, but at this point, the organization has given the necessary support to allow that to happen.

From Big Picture to Classroom

In the course of publishing this book, I have been asked many times who my intended audience is. Whenever I begin discussing organizational structures, I can see teachers make the mental decision to step back from the conversation because they "have no control over stuff like that." But teachers are heavily involved with the hierarchy for two specific, important reasons.

First, all educators in every position play a part in every single level of the hierarchy. Every individual in a school or district plays a role in the creation (or the destruction of) its climate and culture. Every person in a school or district has not only leadership capacity in some role, but also has the choice as to what kind of leader they want to be. Each individual has control over their mindset and their engagement in professional learning. Therefore, while some may say that books on an organizational structure are focused on administration, I would argue that this book very much involves teachers because our organizations *depend on them.*

Second, the organizational structure of the hierarchy can be implemented at a classroom level as well. The one slight change in the foundational levels would be to shift professional learning to personalized learning (see graphic below). However, the ideas of developing a positive climate and culture, effective facilitator and student leaders, and growth and innovator's mindsets that give students the chance to be innovative and divergent thinkers remains the same. By developing procedures and relationships, and by creating brain space for students to learn, we are providing them with this opportunity as well.

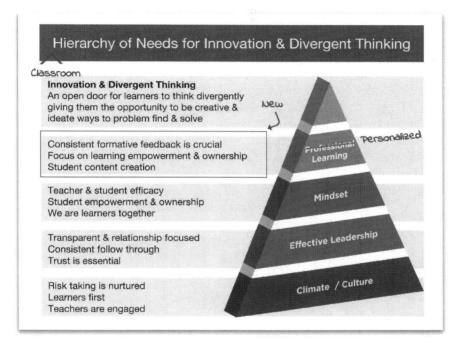

Chapter 1 Summary

It's imperative to define and create a common language, so all stakeholders are working toward the same goals.

Innovation is an idea, concept or product that is new, different, and better. It doesn't need to be something completely new, but can also be a new way to use the original idea. Innovation is a personal journey (adapted from G. Couros *Innovator's Mindset* (2015)).

Divergent Thinking is the ability to recognize our own assumptions, look for limitations, and challenge our own thinking regarding teaching and learning. It's taking an idea and creating new thinking that will facilitate student learning in new, innovative directions for deeper understanding. It is diverging from the norm, challenging current ideas, looking for a variety of solutions, and being willing to learn from failure and grow.

Divergent teachers possess these characteristics:
- Highly reflective
- Voracious learner
- Courageous
- Tenacious
- Mentor

There are a variety of supports that educators need in order to reach the level of thinking divergently and innovatively, many of which have nothing to do with technology.

The foundational levels of climate and culture, effective leadership, mindset, professional learning, and innovative and divergent thinking, when strong and complete, create an atmosphere where teachers are given the headspace to teach innovatively.

Chapter 1 Reflection Questions

The end of each chapter will contain questions aimed at deep reflection, as I believe honest evaluation beginning with oneself and including the organization is the only way that growth can happen. The reflective questions are for your own use, but activities that may aid you in your growth are:

- Blogging about your thoughts on the Hierarchy
- Tweeting one or more things you learned going through the process using #DivergentEDU and tagging @froehlichm
- Creating a short video or blog post discussing one specific change that you'll make resulting from the reflection in this book.

Questions:

1. What is one area that immediately resonated with you in the hierarchy? Why do you think that happened?
2. How supported do you feel in your school? District? Does it vary with different interest areas? For example, do you feel supported in math and reading teaching strategies but wish for more support with technology or

innovative teaching strategies (Genius Hour, Design Thinking, etc.)?

3. What is one area where you feel your school and district excel? What makes that area stand out to you?

4. What is one teaching area in which you excel? How did you get to that point?

5. What holes do you think you have in your foundations?

6. How ready are you to fill the holes in your foundations? What catalyst do you need to drive yourself forward?

Chapter 2
Culture & Climate:
Creating a Common Thread

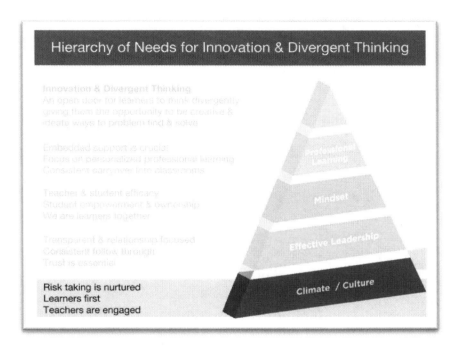

Hierarchy of Needs for Innovation & Divergent Thinking

Innovation & Divergent Thinking
An open door for learners to think divergently,
giving them the opportunity to be creative &
ideate ways to problem find & solve

Embedded support is crucial
Focus on personalized professional learning
Consistent carryover into classrooms

Teacher & student efficacy
Student empowerment & ownership
We are learners together

Transparent & relationship focused
Consistent follow through
Trust is essential

Risk taking is nurtured
Learners first
Teachers are engaged

Professional Learning

Mindset

Effective Leadership

Climate / Culture

I stood in the parking lot of an elementary school on a warm, spring day. To my right, teachers, paraprofessionals, and administration lined up, talking excitedly and placing the legs of severed nylons on their heads. Inside the feet, they had shoved baseballs and tennis balls. To my left, there were plastic bowling pins set up in organized rows. The idea I was told, was to knock down the bowling pins in your row before anyone else knocked down theirs by swinging the weighted stocking with your

head. The teachers then proceeded to Pantyhose
Bowl, complete with whoops and hollers for their
teammates. Ridiculous? Yes. Fun? Totally. Did it
solve some long-standing educational debate on
student achievement? Nope. But it was an
indication of the strong culture and the positive,
collaborative climate of the elementary school. It
was a ritualistic part of their culture that the
teachers would participate once a month in a team-
building exercise. It never took a lot of time because
like all of us, these people had places to be after
school.

This particular time, Pantyhose Bowling
lasted about a half hour and was done right after
students left while teachers were still *on contracted
time.* Although voluntary, most of the staff
participated on a regular basis. It was their way to
connect on a personal level while doing something
that made them laugh and enjoy being in each
other's company.

I drove from that school to another
elementary school that I worked with. Here, the
negative energy could be felt the second that you
entered the building. It was more common to be
ignored by the staff than to be greeted, and you were
more likely to hear gossip as you walked by a
classroom instead of collaboration. Teachers were
despondent and unhappy. Student behaviors were a
major concern, even though the student population
was similar in demographics to the first school. In
this building the established culture was valueless,
and because of the lack of connection to culture, the
climate had become toxic. We often jokingly called

this school the "puppies and rainbows" school, as the leadership would downplay issues instead of creating opportunities for reflection and change. After a half a school year working in this school, I had discovered that I could not be there for more than a few days without being pulled into the dysfunctional vortex myself. So, I would choose to be cognizant of my schedule and not plan too many meetings in a row there. I felt it was a matter of professional survival.

Regarding innovation, the teachers at the first school were on board and ready to go, while the second school's teachers didn't even have the energy to try because they were too busy working on other issues. One school had an established culture and collaborative climate which supported creating relationships, risk-taking, and supporting ideas that endorsed innovation. The other school did not.

Sometimes the terms climate and culture are used interchangeably, but they shouldn't be. If you ask people what each of the terms means, they often have a difficult time articulating their definitions. The culture of a group of people is comprised of the traditions, icons, and shared beliefs amongst the group. It is the established rituals, ceremonies, norms, symbols, stories, shared values, and common understandings that represent the deeper foundation of an organization, and is what everything else, including climate, is built on (Gruenert, 2008). School songs that everyone knows, a mascot whose likeness evokes pride and excitement, and staff birthday celebrations are all examples of culture. A strong culture exists when all stakeholders (administration, teachers, paraprofessionals, custodians, secretaries, students, parents, community members) have made a connection with these ideas and feel like the established culture makes their school a community.

The climate of a building is the attitude, collective mood, and morale of the people who work inside it (Gruenert, 2008). It's the behavior or personality of a building or organization. Sometimes people describe climate as the "feeling" of a particular place when they walk in. Often, to discover the climate of a particular building one needs to do little more than walk into the teacher's lounge. I learned this lesson early on when I was student teaching. I went into the teacher's lounge one time for ten minutes, and after the intolerably negative discussion I heard regarding students and teaching, I never went back.

Culture	Climate
Monday versus Friday	Gives Mondays permission to be miserable
Attitude or mood of the group	Personality of the group
Provides a state of mind	Provides a (limited) way of thinking
Flexible, easy to change	Takes many years to evolve
Based on perceptions	Based on values and beliefs
Feel it when you come in the door	Members cannot feel it
Is all around us	Is part of us
The way we feel around here	The way we do things around here
First step to improvement	Determines if improvement is possible
It's in your head	It's in your head

Taken from School Culture, School Climate:
They are not the same thing by Gruenert (2008)

Although establishing a strong culture lays the foundation, the climate of a building can determine the day-to-day feeling both staff and students get when they come to school. At one point, I was part of a staff meeting where we were expected to put what a positive climate *Looks like, Sounds like, Feels like* onto charts. As I added my answers to the chart paper, I overheard people say things like, "Not working here" and "Take the opposite of this place, and there you go." When everyone was finished, the principal said that we need to work toward what we put on the charts. However, we missed several important pieces of the puzzle. First, there were no positive, established cultural beliefs or rituals, with the exception of birthday treats, that the staff could grab onto. The younger teachers were thirsty for anything to make them feel connected, and the older staff had just given up. Second, the staff was never asked to add what the building *Looks like, Sounds like, and Feels like* currently because the principal was afraid of difficult conversations, so there was no opportunity to look for specific areas of growth. Third, the principal previously established that even though we participated in activities similar to this, nothing was ever done with the information to make improvements in anyone's practice; thus, there was absolutely no buy-in to the process. Not a single person in the room looked at the charts and thought, "What part do I have in this and what changes can I make to improve the way I feel about my students and coming to work every day?" The attitude of the group was that they didn't care because nothing they said or did mattered.

How does a climate where you believe that nothing you say or do matters affect student learning and your attitude regarding innovation and divergence? Will you even bother with the effort it takes to deviate from the norm when it's so difficult just to wrap your mind around what that norm is?

Although climate and culture are two different principles, they do work in tandem. It is difficult to have a positive climate without a strong culture, and generally, a lack of a positive foundational culture results in a negative climate. With time, effort, and strong leadership, a robust culture and positive, collaborative climate can be achieved. Just like a house, you start with the foundation (culture) and build.

Creating a Common Language

Sometimes educators look for that one silver bullet, that one initiative in education that will simultaneously solve all the behavior, curricular, assessment, and technological needs so we can be the rock stars that we desire to be for our students. Many educators continue to search, wide-eyed, for the proverbial silver bullet despite recognizing that teachers have different personalities and teaching styles, that our students are individuals with varying needs, likes, dislikes, desires, motivations, backgrounds, and home lives There isn't one strategy, nor will there ever be one, that will work for all of them. It's like the Catch 22 of education. Even the greatest instructional strategies might really only be effective for a small percentage of students in any given class.

At a district level, I've seen these silver bullet ideas turn into educational jargon that is thrown into mission and vision statements without any common understanding created before doing so. Words and phrases such as "personalized learning" or "innovation" are used to create the most impressive sounding mission and vision statements with the assumption that adding those words in will 1) create an expectation that all teachers are doing those things, and 2) tell the world that the teachers in that district are facilitating their classrooms based on those ideals. The issue with this is that ideally, by placing these words into our mission and vision statements, we are asking teachers to create goals based upon these words. However, if we don't take the time to create a common understanding of what those words mean, we are asking them to create goals based on their own understandings, which might not actually align to what the district believes at all.

An example of this would be a district I worked in that had implanted the word "innovation" into every goal statement and district initiative that they released. Mission and vision statements as well as teacher goals and expectations were littered with the word. At no time, however, was there a common definition created. Therefore, at any point in time, a person could poll ten different people from custodians to administrators (because all should be supporting the mission and vision, right?) and get ten different answers. I did just that and found that I received definitions ranging from "innovation is any learning that is done online" to the better definition of "doing something different." Lacking a common understanding of the word *innovation* would make it difficult for a teacher to meet a goal focusing on being innovative because they don't actually know what exactly they are working toward.

Let's take the two definitions above as an example. The teacher who answered that innovation is any learning that is done online could have been teaching an online class for the last three years where the content of the class has never changed. The content itself could be little more than online worksheets with 50 multiple choice questions as the assessment. The fact that the class hasn't been changed in years suggests that it does not support a definition of being innovative. It is possible at one point that the class was something new and different. However, according to the definition that the teacher constructed, continuing to teach the same class online would be considered innovative.

In the second definition (doing something different), the teacher has always given her fourth-grade students a paper and pencil quiz on the branches of government. She decides that this year she is going to use Thinglink (www.thinglink.com) to have her students upload a photo that represents the three branches and then add additional text, photos, and video to each branch describing the duties performed by each. The assessment is something new and different for her, and she has fit the definition that she believes to be innovation.

In taking a look at these two scenarios from the teachers' perspective, they were both fulfilling the goal of providing students with what they thought were innovative learning opportunities, but are they both meeting the district's expectation of what innovation is? If the district has not created a common understanding of what the word means, the teachers will either do their best to come up with a reasonable definition, or they will retrofit the word and their definition to whatever they are already doing. Either way, in the absence of the district explicitly defining a term, people will create their own meaning and, in the process, will likely end up with multiple different definitions, none of which may be correct.

In another example, I worked with a district that defined personalized learning as "creating personalized pathways for students." Their personalized pathways meant that if a student had severe behavior challenges or there was a learning style that wasn't best suited for the classroom, the student(s) were pulled out into programs in a separate school to meet their needs. This was the district's definition of personalized learning, which differs from my definition of it being a pedagogical approach where all students feel empowered and are taught to take ownership of their learning. If I were a new teacher or administrator in that district and created a goal based on my own definition of personalized learning, I would be working toward a goal that would not align to the district's vision of personalized learning. For both parties, this doesn't work. As a new teacher, I wouldn't feel supported in my goal because the district is not going to be providing resources to meet my definition; from the district's standpoint, I'm not meeting the goal because it doesn't align with the practices of their definition. The lack of communication and definition creates a lose-lose situation.

Recently, I was presenting a workshop on personalized learning where I gave participants a word that I wanted them to define and asked the teachers to close their devices briefly so they couldn't look up the definition. The word was "nomophobia." Teachers were asked to define the word, create a SMART (specific, measurable, attainable, relevant, time-bound) goal to meet the needs for an initiative being handed down about nomophobia, and action steps on how to meet the SMART goal. The results were amazing. Teachers created very real goals and definitions. They had an idea of what the word could be by noticing that the root word "phobia" was there, similar to how we might have an idea of what a buzzword might mean. They created action steps that would be best practice for meeting any goal. They developed sessions of professional learning, students were creating content based on the sessions, teachers were running PLCs based on the concept. They had so many activities that we see in new districtwide and schoolwide implementations every day. When all the groups finished, we looked at how they defined the unknown word. Even though they created fantastically realistic goals, activities, implementation plans, and professional learning opportunities, all of their definitions, although similar, were incorrect. All of them had an element of truth. The groups recognized that phobia was a fear, but the root word threw them off. Therefore, while the plans were solid, nobody knew what the goals and activities were really accomplishing. Now granted, they weren't allowed to look the definition up, but realistically, how often is substantial research done on a concept before the word being thrown into our everyday education language?

Nomophobia, by the way, is the fear of being without a mobile phone. I am a self-diagnosed nomophobiac because I have a difficult time being away from my phone. The term they needed to

define and create their implementation plans had
nothing to do with education at all, yet they were
able to completely integrate it into our hypothetical
everyday learning.

Moving forward from that activity, in order
to create a common understanding for our
workshop on personalized learning, the teachers
broke into groups, read articles on personalized
learning that were curated by me as well as some
they found on their own. Then they were asked to
write the most important ideas that related to
personalized learning on to a shared document.
From there, the group crafted a definition of what
personalized learning meant based on the research
that was used. It took about an hour and a half in
the six-hour workshop to develop the definition
from start to finish, but for the rest of the day, we
referred back to what we had created. Furthermore,
the definition was deconstructed and applied to
classroom learning. Everyone in the workshop had
complete buy-in into the definition because they
had been a part of creating it, and as they worked
on activities throughout the rest of the workshop,
they measured what they had created against the
definition to see if it fit. By taking the time to create
a definition for what we were trying to work toward,
everyone was given the same foundation, skills, and
knowledge they needed to effectively develop
activities that aligned to our overall beliefs on
personalized learning.

Since the first time I did the workshop, I
have done this activity surrounding creating a
common language with many different districts. I

have never gone to one that had major key terms in their mission and vision or goal statements defined. In asking groups of people to define the terms in their mission, vision, and goal statements, I have never come across people- even within the same group, who had the same understanding as to what the terms meant (i.e., a group of administrators broken into smaller groups came up with different definitions for their mission vocabulary). This lack of communication can leave people feeling like they're in the dark, while on the flip side, creating a common language can give people something that they can grasp onto in the culture of their school or district. Defining the terms empowers them to recognize and take ownership of the culture. When done correctly, it is one simple way to strengthen a culture.

There are multiple reasons why taking the time to define a word takes a backseat to just moving forward with an initiative. Taking the time to define a word can seem like an elementary task, but as teachers when we begin a new unit, we often first provide students with definitions to vocabulary words that they may encounter as they read. Usually, we ask them to find the definitions, write them on flashcards or use Quizlet (www.quizlet.com) to help them practice, and even possibly assess them on their understanding of the vocabulary words. Why do we do this? Because we want students to have background knowledge of the words that pertain to the overarching concept of the unit. We want them to be able to make connections to both other content areas and their own lives, and to be able to understand fully what they are researching. We want to provide them with a base of knowledge as they move forward in their learning, similar to how we should create these common definitions with teachers, so they can then work towards goals they will then understand.

Sometimes I think we might not take the time to define things because we either assume that all stakeholders already have a clear understanding, or we are afraid that our definition of a concept is wrong. Taking the time to craft common understandings alleviates the stress and uncertainty of working toward a goal that isn't understood or worse, implementing incorrect strategies or misunderstandings in the classroom.

In order to truly create a culture of innovation, everyone involved in student learning must have a common understanding of what the district's mission and vision are, and be able to implement ideas and lessons matching the concept in their positions. At any point, any person in any position in the district should be able to define concepts that the district has deemed important to student learning. Assuming that people can define the terms on their own is not nearly focused enough to truly expect that those concepts are being implemented according to the intentions of the district.

Taking the time to create a common language can seem like a meaningless, mundane task, but it is actually a crucial practice that gives all stakeholders the information they need to create goals that align with district philosophies. It is a practice that has been in place with teaching students for years, providing the definitions to unknown vocabulary words that are needed to understand content, and it's unreasonable to assume that teachers, because they are professionals, know the district's definition of a concept, no matter how widely it has been discussed in the education field.

Best Practices for Creating a Common Language

If you find terms that haven't been defined in the mission, vision, or teacher goals, or even commonly used terms that are aligned with initiatives like Continuous Improvement, here are some best practices for building those definitions:

- **Get buy-in from all stakeholders:** Have a small group of representation from all stakeholders on a team that defines the terms. The cross representation will help assure everyone's voices are heard.
- **Wordsmith:** Play with the words in the definition. Look up synonyms. Step away from the definition and come back to it. Be sure it conveys what is intended. How will the definition possibly be interpreted by those who were not a part of the creation?
- **Short and memorable:** Create definitions that can be easily recited by keeping them short. The idea behind the common language is that anyone in the district should be able to

recite it. Long, extensive, and wordy definitions will get lost. Nobody is going to carry around their district-issued common language dictionary.

- **Keep the list short, too:** The list of words that are defined should be the ones that are most important. If you go longer than one page of words and definitions, you have too many for people to attempt to remember. You want the list and the definitions to be something that people gravitate toward and give them a common thread. You don't want to make it frustrating to try to remember.

- **Listen:** Once the words have been adopted by the staff, listen for discrepancies in how they are used. Be certain that once the definitions have been created, they are being used correctly.

Cultivating a Shared Belief System

Probably one of the most impressive displays of creating shared beliefs I have witnessed happened in another school I worked in that same year. The math and literacy instructional support teachers participated in a book study on *Read, Write, Lead: breakthrough strategies for schoolwide literacy success* by Regie Routman (2014). To find the common beliefs among the staff regarding literacy, math, and student learning, they constructed statements and then had staff anonymously vote on if they agreed with the statement or not. For example, one statement might be, "all students can learn." If 100% of the staff agreed that all students can learn, the statement would be hung up in the vestibule of the school. If there were even one teacher who disagreed, there would be professional reading and development in the statement's area. Then, mid-year, the staff would be given the list of statements again, and the process would continue. Newly shared beliefs would be added and hung as a declaration of the progress and unity of the staff.

What if all schools did this, but we included statements like, "I will try new, innovative ideas in my teaching," or, "I know it's okay to fail as I'm trying something new because I know I can learn from that failure to improve my practice?" If either of these were a shared belief amongst the staff, the atmosphere would be ripe for change. Similar to the discussion as to why creating a common language puts everyone on the same page, creating common understandings and a shared belief system regarding innovation does the same. Imagine a teacher's comfort level rising as they realize that everyone around them believes and supports innovative teaching practices, that they also will be stepping outside their comfort zone, and they might need a pep talk if it fails. All of a sudden trying something new doesn't seem so terrifying when everyone is working toward the same goals.

Be Explicit About Expectations and Procedures

As an elementary teacher, I absolutely loved the book *The First Days of School* (Wong and Wong, 1991). My students and I would spend a large portion of the beginning of the year establishing the expectations (for both myself and for them), and practicing the procedures so they would know how the classroom worked. Nothing was left to assumption. I was often questioned by colleagues why I took so much time working on these things because, at the beginning of the year, my class would often fall behind the curricular timeline that had been established by my grade level peers. But by creating a culture where students and I could consistently be on the same page, we were able to exceed what we needed to learn.

I invested so fully in taking the time to establish this type of culture because I believe students feel more secure and comfortable in an environment where they know what is expected of them and how to get the day-to-day stuff done. I established that I trusted the students by involving them in some of the decisions regarding procedures. When they inevitably asked to be able to go to the bathroom when they needed to, I proved I trusted my fourth and fifth graders by allowing them to take the bathroom pass and go when they needed to go *without asking permission first.* When we came upon a situation where we didn't have an established procedure, we would create one together (I would usually ask, "What procedure would work best for you?"), practice it, and move on. As a result, the students in my class could focus on their learning because they knew what their classmates and I expected of them, and they knew the procedures for anything logistical that they needed to do.

I believe this same idea holds true for staff members. Sometimes, because teachers are professionals, we assume that they know what the procedures and expectations are, but that's not necessarily true. It's possible that they have not been told, or if they might interpret situations around them differently than they are intended. Especially in the case of either a lack of culture or high turnover (which might go hand in hand), the expectations and procedures need to be so clearly established that even the newest of staff members could tell a visitor "how things work" in their school. If these concepts are currently absent from the school, take time to talk to staff about what they need to look like. Some questions to ask are:

- What do staff meetings look like? (e.g., be on time, bring your device, end on time)
- What is the difference between meetings and professional learning, and what happens at each?
- What is the expectation for collaboration between staff members? How about shared professional practice?
- How do we ask for support when we need help trying something new or innovative?
- What process do we go through if we find a procedure or policy that isn't working?

When teachers know what to expect and know the established procedures will be honored, they will have the comfort level needed to branch out and begin to think about their teaching and learning in different ways. If teachers are constantly anxiety-ridden because they don't know what to expect from minute to minute, they are less likely to have the capacity or motivation to change anything they do because they will consistently feel like they are just keeping their heads above water. Not only does this lead to an unhappy, unhealthy learning climate, but it doesn't lead to innovative thinking or divergent teaching practices.

To institute these common understandings, set up a time where as a staff, they can be created and decided. Write them down. Make it clear that it is everyone's responsibility to both follow the procedures and encourage everyone around them to do the same. By creating them as a group, there will be more buy-in to the process. Be careful, however, to stay away from compliance measures that take freedoms away from teachers. It's important to stick to procedures and expectations that instead give teachers confidence in the logistical parts of their day, so they can focus on student learning and moving their own practice forward.

Chapter 2 Summary

Culture is the traditions, icons, and shared beliefs among a group of people. It is the established rituals, ceremonies, norms, symbols, stories, shared values and common understandings that represent the deeper foundation of an organization, and is what everything else, including climate, is built on (Gruenert, 2008).

Climate is the behavior or personality of a building or organization. Sometimes, people describe climate as the "feeling" of a particular place when they walk in. The climate of a building is the attitude, collective mood, and morale of the people who work inside it (Gruenert, 2008).

Creating a common language defines terms for all stakeholders. This accomplishes the following:
Everyone is working toward the same common goals.
People do not need to wonder if they're doing things "right" according to the district.
It creates unity among stakeholders and gives them language to bind them together.

Best practices for creating a common language are to bring together a team, wordsmith the memorable definitions, and keep the list short. Continue implementation by listening for understanding.

Creating common values ensures everyone is working for the same common good and holds certain beliefs in high regard.

Creating common understandings relieves stress from teachers by providing necessary procedures and norming behavior.

Chapter 2 Reflection Questions

1. List and define one to two terms regularly used in your district that may not be defined for stakeholders. These could be being used in initiatives, your mission/vision, etc.
2. How will you explicitly and effectively communicate these definitions to stakeholders?
3. What do you see as values you desire your district to have? School? Classroom?
4. What do you see as what your district/school/classroom actually valuing (how do those compare)?
5. What specifically do you do (or not do) that proves those are the values?
6. What values do your initiatives support?

Chapter 3:

The Feels of Climate and Culture

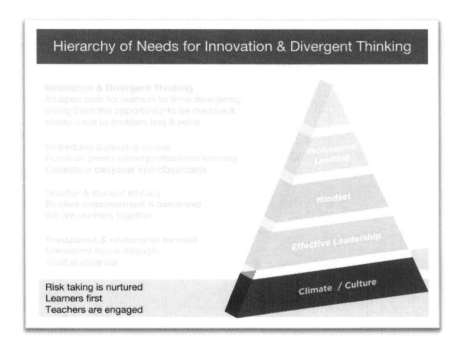

Relationships Determine Success

Every interaction we have with others will create a relationship for better or worse. Focusing on the little actions we take to create positive relationships is imperative because the relationships we have will affect every single interaction we have going forward. Cultivating positive relationships will result in moving toward a supportive, collaborative, and innovative climate. When connections are established, people feel more comfortable taking risks because they know they will be supported if they fail. They will freely share their ideas and stories of triumphant lessons because they know they will not be judged, and they have a strong desire to see the people around them succeed. People are less likely to disagree with someone they have established a professional relationship with, but if they do happen, disagreements can be worked through more positively when the participants trust and respect each other.

It's important to note that the kind of relationships I'm referring to are the ones where an actual connection is made. You might have a positive relationship with the tenth-grade English teacher across the building that you see once every three weeks because you think she's nice and you say hello in the hall, but you might not have made a personal connection to this person. If they moved to a different building you might not think twice about it. We need to create allies in learning with the people around us, and feel like we are moving forward together as a team to truly create an environment where we feel safe in attempting to move outside our comfort zones.

One way to establish those kinds of connections, as the story of the Pantyhose Bowling went, is to create opportunities for staff members to have fun. There is often a lack of importance put on the idea of having fun, like it is something extra that really doesn't have a function in the workplace. The depth of personal connections made while participating in an activity that results in laughter and playfulness can't be replicated just by saying hello in the hall or sitting in a meeting. When genuine connections have been made, the level of trust and support felt by everyone around will establish the culture and climate necessary for innovative and divergent thinking and practices.

Opportunities for Improvement in Climate and Culture

Teacher engagement

So many times we discuss teacher engagement in the form of how engrossed teachers are in their professional learning. However, I've realized that teacher engagement has more to do with the depth of the relationship that an educator still feels they have with their profession than it does their professional learning. I believe that the level of engagement and efficacy educators feel in our profession directly correlates to how happy we are in our jobs and subsequently the passion we exhibit when we teach.

Educator disengagement is stronger than just not being interested in what you are learning or teaching at the time. It's the complete disconnection to the *why* behind teaching. And disengagement is a serious issue. It gives people's minds the opportunity and permission to do things like incessantly complain about students' laziness, roll their eyes at the teachers who are excited and still engaged, and either do anything they can to work against the administration or just do nothing exciting to fly under the radar. Sometimes the teachers who are the most disengaged expect the highest level of engagement out of their disengaged students, even though they don't feel that connection themselves.

Few professions require as much passion and dedication as being an educator. Our focus needs to be children and what we can do to support them in becoming the best versions of themselves. We work tirelessly, lose sleep, and spend more time with other people's children than we do our own. But, year after year, we are required to do more with less. Classroom budgets dwindle while expectations rise, declining quality of health insurances leave us with more bills for general care, yet our salaries rarely go up, and new challenging behaviors and mental health issues surfacing in both teachers and kids wear educators down.

Even though I would say that I'm highly engaged in my profession now, I wasn't immune to this issue.

My first teaching job was a one-year, limited term, emergency licensure contract where I taught Human Growth and Development (HG&D) and Family and Consumer Education to middle school students. It was pure baptism by fire. I had never taught HG&D and I was a terrible cook, but this position taught me some of what would become my most basic beliefs about education. Very few other teaching experiences will highlight the extreme need for relationship building like teaching HG&D at the middle school level, and my ability to build relationships became one of my most valuable assets. Also, there are few other age levels of students that will keep you mentally on your toes like middle schoolers. It's difficult to find another grade level with the quirkiness, wannabe adult-like childishness of a middle schooler. I was able to develop my abilities to be quick-witted and to be flexible to accept times when lessons needed to change according to their needs. The fact that I didn't actually know how to cook forced me to learn along with students. When I failed at even teaching them the correct way to make omelets and the resulting omelets tasted all kinds of wrong, I learned how to laugh at myself (and allow my students to see my reaction when I fail). Most importantly, I developed an absolute devotion for teaching, which turned into a complete love and passion for the profession when I originally thought it was just going to be a job.

I specifically remember discussing the topic of teacher burnout with a colleague in my second year of teaching. I told them that could never happen to me because I loved my job too much.

Fast forward to when I had been teaching for about five years and I became stuck...stuck in the everyday grind of attempting to keep up with pacing and assessments, politics of the school and district, new initiatives with little to no support, and the desire to be the best teacher for my students, but even tired of my own ideas. School began to feel exhausting instead of invigorating, and I increasingly was looking more forward to the weekends than I had in the past. I knew I wanted to move forward, but I didn't know how to get there. I was at the pivotal point where I think some teachers begin to disengage from their students and profession.

When I hit this point in my career, I began to say things like:

"If the district is not going to do _____ for me, they can't expect me to do _____ for them."

"(student's name) is doing that to me on purpose just to irritate me."

"I'm not doing _____ because the district doesn't pay me to do that."

I was so incredibly tired of being told that I needed to know my students the best but then told to follow the adopted canned curriculum with fidelity. I was terrified of becoming the person who cared more about compliance and content than about my students and relationships. I was hurt, and I didn't feel trusted with my professional decisions that I had partially made with a very personal heart. I had checked out, and I felt I was done. I like to tell myself that my students didn't notice because, for me, it wasn't the students but the politics of education that disengaged me. But that's probably not true. They probably knew. And even though I had the sweetest, most hard-working class of my career, the last year I was in the classroom I couldn't pull myself back into the groove to even really appreciate it. It's seriously one of my biggest professional regrets- when the students don't feel like we care even when they're struggling (especially when they're struggling), we have truly failed as educators.

At first, I thought I was just in a district that wasn't providing me with what I needed to be the teacher I was destined to be, which might have been true- but only to a point. However, after moving districts to become a technology integrator, I realized the actual issue was something I didn't necessarily want to admit. The issue was inside me. It took me taking control of the way that I viewed my profession through deep and sometimes difficult reflection to get to where I am today.

It took me many years to learn how to deeply reflect. I learned to ask myself questions like:

- What could I have done differently in that situation to change the outcome?
- How does this situation or person make me feel? What is the root of that feeling? How can I work with that or change it?
- Am I being reasonable in my expectations of others? Am I being reasonable in my expectations for myself?
- How are my own personal biases affecting this situation? My decisions? The outcome?

There are so many positives that come from being truly engaged in your profession. I am less stressed. I am a better leader and educator. I appreciate students and the quirks that make them special. I am more open to diverse opinions and ideas. I know my value. I recognize the value in others. I know my place in the education world. Most importantly, I am happy.

The continuum of engagement

Having been disengaged from the profession before, I feel like I can talk about it with some degree of expertise, even if that expertise is only because I experienced it and beat it. As a result, I often watch for signs or symptoms of teachers being disengaged because I do feel that part of my job is a responsibility to help teachers either stay engaged or remember why they began teaching in the first place. There's a continuum of disengagement. You are not either engaged or disengaged. It reminds me a bit of the process by which people grieve. Even though grief is a similar process and certain stages can be predicted, the actual course it takes can be different for everybody.

I think people assume that you are either happy or not happy in your job. And if you look at a continuum, many people may place happy and then sad or angry at the opposite ends of the spectrum. Even if you want to say you love your job, some may place hate at the opposite end. But I don't believe either of these to be true. I think that the opposite of happy or love is instead, apathy. When you are sad or angry it means that you are still passionate, and you care. I believe this to be true about many things, not just the engagement you feel in teaching. I feel like it's true about life in general.

When you feel numb towards something and no longer care, you have truly, completely lost your *why*. And if you're speaking in regard to emotion toward teaching, I'd most love to be happy, but my second choice would be to be angry because I would know that I still feel passionate enough to fight for what I believe. Apathy on the other hand, is a hopeless, lost feeling. And if you feel like nothing you do matters, where would you even get the energy to try?

The causes of disengagement

I feel like many of us can think about someone who fits this description even if we don't feel this way ourselves. How do people get this way? I think there are a few possibilities as to what brings this on, but part of the difficulty of "solving" the issue is that it's so deeply personal to whoever is experiencing it. That's why the best prevention is self-awareness and knowing if you're beginning to fall into the trap.

Personal hurt

Sometimes what emotionally removes people from education has nothing to do with education at all. It may be a personal trauma or adversity that requires a person's full attention that draws them away. The emotion of the personal situation is either so deeply hurtful or takes place over an extended period of time (or both), and educators struggle to get back into the groove and find their happy teaching place again.

Professional hurt

One of the biggest takeaways I had from Rick Jetter and Rebecca Coda's book *Escaping the School Leader's Dunk Tank* (2016) was that when we suffer adversity in the workplace, it emotionally hurts us. We become a little more disheartened every time it happens. Sometimes, it's simply about having more put on our plates than any one person can be expected to do. It could also be workplace bullying (which can come in the form of colleagues, parents, administration), or from an administrator or colleagues who are against risk-taking, or from policies that are compliance-based and stifle creativity and innovation. Even a lack of trust for the people around you can cause hurt. While personal resiliency varies, everyone will have a threshold that when they reach it, they may give up. Even the most resilient people have a breaking point, and reaching that point may cause them to become disengaged.

Burnout

Sometimes, we overuse the term burnout. We say things like, "I'm so burnt out after the tough week." But professional burnout is absolutely a real thing, and one of the feelings that true burnout can lead to is detachment. Psychology Today posted the article The Teacher Burnout Epidemic (Grant Rankin, 2016) on teacher burnout which included data that said:

About half a million (15% of) U.S. teachers leave the profession every year (Seidel, 2014).

More than 41% of teachers leave the profession within five years of starting, and teacher attrition has risen significantly over the last two decades (Ingersoll, Merrill, and Stuckey, 2014). This provides clarification to Ingersoll's (2012) oft-cited estimate that 40%-50% of new teachers leave within their first five years on the job.

TNTP (formerly The New Teacher Project) reported almost 66% of the nation's best teachers continue to leave the profession for careers elsewhere (Chartock & Wiener, 2014).

It is clear our teachers are struggling, but we should refrain from placing the blame on them. Rather, consider the demands and unsustainability of the job.

. . .teachers are less likely to be able to deliver high-quality instruction when they are not able to decompress (Neufeld, 2014). Stressed, overworked, frustrated teachers are less able to connect in positive ways with students and to offer students the best instruction.

Some of the symptoms of burnout include (Bourg Carter, 2012):

- Consistently being emotionally and physically exhausted accompanied with dread of what might happen the next day
- Impaired concentration that can get worse the longer it continues
- Weakened immune system (i.e., you get sick easier)

- Other mental health issues like anxiety or depression
- In the beginning, constant irritability and later, angry outbursts

Many of the symptoms of burnout can affect both a person's personal and professional life. Identifying when you need support and focusing in on stressors is important for dealing with burnout. Also, knowing when to take control of your own attitude is imperative. If you're feeling cynical at work, for example, find ways to improve your mindset. Begin looking for the small wins and positives throughout the day to boost your mood. Celebrate your accomplishments and those of others.

Secondary Traumatic Stress

Secondary traumatic stress (STS) (also known as compassion fatigue or vicarious trauma), as discussed in my book *The Fire Within: Lessons from defeat that have ignited a passion for learning* (2018), is when people who hear of other's trauma and who work with others who have experienced trauma and exhibit trauma behaviors, begin to develop the symptoms of Post-Traumatic Stress Disorder (PTSD) even if they have never suffered a trauma themselves. The chart below is from the Administration for Children and Families (n.d.) and shows the symptoms to look for:

Cognitive	Emotional
Lowered Concentration	Guilt
Apathy	Anger
Rigid thinking	Numbness
Perfectionism	Sadness
Preoccupation with trauma	Helplessness
Behavioral	**Physical**
Withdrawal	Increased heart rate
Sleep disturbance	Difficulty breathing
Appetite change	Muscle and joint pain
Hyper-vigilance	Impaired immune system
Elevated startle response	Increased severity of medical concerns

Secondary traumatic stress and burnout have both similar symptoms and ways to cope. For both, it's important to recognize when you need professional help.

Regardless of the reason for disengagement, the most important step to take is developing self-awareness and being mindful of how you feel to catch it in the early stages. I want people to understand that these feelings are real, and they are not weird or terrible teachers for having them, but there is an underlying cause of their disengagement. Many times, I find that educators who are disengaged aren't necessarily truly happy people, at least not in their profession. I believe it is so much more rewarding to love your job, what you do, and in turn, the students you teach. Your students will be better people for it, and that's really why many got into education in the first place.

If you reach the point of apathy, I don't think all is lost. I definitely don't believe that you need to necessarily leave the profession. We lose phenomenal teachers every day who conclude that they no longer love teaching the way they should because we either don't recognize disengagement or we feel too guilty and embarrassed to talk about it. Reigniting the flame for learning and loving what you do may just take a little bit more time. One of the most important steps is being open, and talking to somebody about it can help. Blogging, finding a passion, or taking up a new interest in education are a few things that can bring a teacher back into loving what they do. Doing mental body scans, paying attention to your physical and emotional well-being to catch it early, and using self-care are all important steps as well. Blaming others and being angry will not help. Give yourself and the profession a clean slate. The reconnection is not immediate, but the same resilience and grit we ask our kids to employ every day will help get you there. It took me about eight months to figure out why I had gotten into education again after I figured out I wanted to leave. But the time and the effort it took was so worth it.

Strategies to re-engage

Ultimately, I had to make the decision within myself to re-engage. The most important one I made, however, was the decision to just be better.

I knew that for me to love education again, the changes had to start with me.

I practiced reflecting and developed my core beliefs

My reflective thinking shifted from what other people had done to me to what I could have done better. I stopped focusing on the fact that sometimes other people's decisions affected the outcome of something I was doing, and started focusing on what I could have done differently in the situation. When I realized that I had more control over my world than I thought I did, I was able to drive myself forward in spite of what others were doing around me and focus on the people that were willing to support me instead.

My practice in reflection continued when I started blogging but really didn't develop until I realized that my blog was about my own reflection for me, and not writing for someone else. It was about getting my own thoughts in order to create headspace and develop my core beliefs, which I'll discuss more in the chapter on mindset.

I grew my PLN

I have wholeheartedly recognized that I am only as good as the people I surround myself with. I have worked hard to connect with people that are amazing at what they do. I have multiple mentors because everyone has different strengths and can help me improve in those areas. I have a wide range of people I've connected with to the point that at any given time with any question I have, I know multiple people I could reach out to that would help me, and I have complete faith in their abilities to do so. I have used Twitter mainly to grow my PLN, but I've also utilized Facebook, Instagram, and LinkedIn, as well as connected in person with people at conferences. I've focused on growing my PLN worldwide because I want to be challenged by a wider range of ideas and opinions.

I focused on relationships

One strength I have is creating relationships, and if you're growing your PLN, relationships still need to be at the forefront. It's not enough to be connected with them virtually or superficially, the relationships created in these places need to be cultivated and nurtured. Like any relationship, it takes time and effort. I do the same with the people around me. People often tell me, "I feel like I have a connection to you," but it's really just because I legitimately care and will do whatever I can for the people I care about. Minimal effort into relationships will result in minimal connection and minimal support from others. People can sense when they are not valued as important, especially if they perceive someone as connecting with them only when they need assistance.

I read books

After college, I stopped reading professional books because the ones assigned to us in classes were difficult and unengaging. I didn't understand that not all professional books were like that. I began setting a reading goal of reading for myself, just like I asked my students to do. I also had a long commute, so I would find audiobooks to listen to. I looked for books that fit particular purposes and what I needed at that moment. Sometimes it was a book that would push my thinking, sometimes it was one that would support my thinking, and sometimes it was professional literature that would motivate or inspire me. Prior to re-engaging, I would focus on non-fiction books and "fun reading," but I began to understand that there is a place for both, and if I want to continue growing, I need to connect with great thinkers and authors in the education field.

When I realized that I no longer wanted to be miserable going to work every day, that I owed my students so much better than I was, and that I had control over how I viewed and engaged in my profession, I finally discovered the educator I was meant to be. It wasn't going to be a degree or a district that gave that to me, I needed to go out and take control of what that looked and felt like. It was me that had to make that decision and take the initiative, and it'll always be one of the best decisions I've ever made for both myself and the little people I work with every day.

How engagement affects climate and culture

Engaged teachers do what they can to provide a positive climate and strong culture for their students and colleagues. They are always learning, reflecting, and looking for ways to improve their practice or help others. They know that everything they do affects the people around them and they strive to be the person they would want to work with.

Disengaged teachers exhibiting negativity or apathy can bring down even the most positive of climates. They are often found complaining about adults and students around them and the amount of work they have. Sometimes their concerns are totally legitimate. Just because they're disengaged doesn't mean that they're wrong about how they feel. However, I've found that the more they complain, the less people listen to them because their true concerns get lost within the vast array of topics they're upset about. And unfortunately, negativity breeds negativity. Disengaged teachers are also less likely to participate in activities meant to build a strong culture, and if they do, it's usually met with reluctance on their part. They are also less likely to put the time in that's necessary to grow their repertoire of innovative teaching strategies or develop even an interest in divergent thought.

It is important to recognize that disagreeing with a compliance measure or initiative does not necessarily mean a teacher is disengaged. Engaged teachers are passionate about their calling and may promote the system that they think is best for students. It's also important to recognize that disengagement is not an excuse, nor can it be used to ignore the pleas of engaged teachers by assuming they're disengaged. The only way to know the difference is to build a culture of relationship building and procedures for disagreements to be heard appropriately.

Foundations of Trust

Trust should be the concrete foundation of a relationship, and yet it can also be the reason that the relationship ends or is in constant question. When I speak with employees about why they are unhappy (doesn't matter if it's private or public sector), a lack of trust for leaders or their colleagues is often recounted as one of the main reasons that they feel unsupported. Trust is imperative for a supportive culture and positive, collaborative climate. There are so many ways that trust can be broken besides an untruth. I think sometimes it can happen without us even realizing it until it's too late because it can happen incrementally with little actions that break the bonds over time.

I want to trust you to keep me informed

I've often found that a lack of transparency can lead to feelings of distrust. When people feel that there is more information needed to make a decision, or to know the *why* behind a decision, they tend to feel like it's possible that the information was intentionally hidden. This can be made worse if a decision was made that fails and subsequent data or information is released that doesn't support the original decision. When details are missing, people wonder why and trust in the people making those decisions can be shaky. Withholding important information will often be seen at the same level as a blatant lie because both are done intentionally.

If there is already a foundation of distrust, more transparency is necessary to rebuild it. When people trust decision-makers and leaders, they are confident that they are doing their jobs to the best of their ability and making decisions that will support teachers and students. If trust is broken in any capacity, opaque transparency will only frustrate people and leave them doubting the decisions made.

I want to trust you to try your hardest

In having a conversation with my friend Rodney Turner (@TechyTurner), he told me, "You can't place your own expectations on people's actions and then get disappointed when they don't live up to them. Your expectations are yours alone." I found that when I had high expectations for someone and they didn't rise to meet them, I would begin to feel like I couldn't trust that they were doing everything they could to create a successful situation. I would begin to not trust that they would ever do it, and therefore not trust the person. Knowing this has made me more cognizant of the expectations I have for people and if they are reasonable because in this case, this is more my problem and less of theirs. I have also been reflecting on if my expectations were general or if I have made them higher because of the person's relationship to me; would I place the same expectations on myself if I were in that situation? I try to be aware, however, that just because I deem them as reasonable and appropriate, it still doesn't necessarily make my expectations right.

These types of expectations are, of course, different than having high expectations for student learning and embracing the knowledge that someone has the ability to be amazing. That should never change.

I want to trust you to be consistent

Along with expectations, trust can be created by being as close to your real self as possible all the time. When we meet people, work with them, begin to trust and know them, we begin to pick out certain aspects of their personality that are constant. When those traits unexpectedly change, or a decision is made that doesn't jive with previous decisions, we start to not only mistrust the person but to question their reliability. I personally really struggle with people who have unreliable personalities where I never know what I'm going to get when I talk to them from day to day. The more constant and reliable someone is, the more likely we are to trust them because we know what to expect all the time. The problem is when they waiver from reassuring consistency. The more consistent their personality, the more an off decision or act will give the feeling of whiplash. On the flip side, someone whose only consistency is being inconsistent may never have the trust that is needed because people don't know what to expect from them.

<u>I want to trust you to do what you say you will</u>

Follow through might be one of the most important aspects of trust, especially if trust has been broken at some point. When people know that you'll stand behind your word, they are more likely to trust that whatever needs to get done will get done. Also, the quality of follow-through matters. If a task is accomplished only half-way or with little effort, trust will begin to waver as people will wonder why it couldn't have been done right the first time.

<u>I want to trust you believe in the things you ask me to do</u>

People often place a high amount of value on what they choose to spend their time on. Therefore, when they're asked to spend their time on an idea or implementation, they generally want to know the reasons behind that, and rightfully so. The problem comes in when they are asked to do something that is not being modeled for them, which brings on the question, "why is it important for me to spend my time on it, but not that person?" This makes people leery of the person assigning the task. When this is done repeatedly, it can lead to distrust.

Opportunities for Building Trust are in the Things We Do and Don't Do

I believe it is human nature to want to trust people, but it's definitely a feeling that when broken, takes a great deal of time to mend. It's imperative that we have trust in the people around us for support, kindness, empathy, and collaboration. Many times, we associate the breaking of trust with something someone does *to us*. Their words or actions cause us to feel betrayed. For example, if your principal says they support risk-taking, but then chastise you for a failed lesson attempt, the trust that risk-taking is safe is broken. It's like an action causes a reaction, and that reaction is distrust.

I also believe, however, that distrust can also be earned by not doing. The lack of action can cause just as much of a wave in a relationship (personal or professional) as an action.

Do what you say you're going to do

If you've ever uttered the phrase "I'll believe it when I see it," about someone, you've lost trust in that person to finish what they say they will do. A repeated lack of follow-through can cause trust to dwindle with every occurrence. The lack of action can be anything from not finishing assigned collaborations to not being available for support when needed. It can even be in the perception of someone not doing their job when their lack of assistance or attention affects the way that you do your job.

Anticipate others' needs

We obviously cannot anticipate everyone's needs all the time, but I do believe that in this area, people will award points for effort when they feel that the majority of the time people are being proactive versus reactive. Reactiveness causes anxiety and stress for many people and can cause a person to wonder why an avoidable situation couldn't be seen coming. Regarding trust, if I feel a person relies more on reactiveness than proactiveness, I may feel like I need to be more on point to catch situations because I don't trust them to anticipate the needs of people around them.

Speak up when it matters

We can say a great deal with silence. We can cause just as much distrust when we don't say anything when someone expects us to have their back. If it happens repeatedly, the distrust may run so deep that they may question if the support will ever be given.

However, this support also includes the ability to have challenging conversations with people who need to improve their practice; not only the positive, feel-good support but holding people accountable as well.

A clear example of this occurred in the school where the principal refused to focus any energy on the issues that were plaguing the climate and culture of the building. Instead, she would point out only the good things that were happening while ignoring the lack of positive relationships or accountability for everyone in the building. This caused a major distrust of her. The staff began to understand that bringing issues to her attention only ended in disappointment from her lack of action. Therefore, they began handling issues themselves which contributed to the negative climate and lack of a strong, positive culture.

Remembering that our words and actions, or lack thereof, convey a powerful message as well is imperative when taking a purposeful approach to leadership and communication with the people around us. Trust can be broken in an instant and takes patience, diligence, and dependability in order to rebuild.

Rebuilding Trust

The easiest way to maintain trust is, of course, to never lose it in the first place. I've found this is difficult (although not impossible) for two reasons: first, people perceive situations in such different ways and second, sometimes distrust is inherited with the position. I've found this to be true with administration especially. If a former principal was not trusted, it would take the new principal much longer to gain the trust of the staff even though they themselves have never broken the trust of the staff. There is rarely a clean slate given to a new person because feelings of distrust can be tied to the perception of a position versus an actual person. While this might seem unfair, it's important for a new principal (in this case) to recognize the issue, accept it, and do what they can to rebuild the trust.

Building trust in challenging conversations

Educators are taught to be positive, complementary, and to give feedback that people can feel good about and helps them grow. What we often miss though, is the importance of having challenging conversations. I see this most often with administrators, but it is certainly a problem across the board. Teachers too, need to be able to have conversations with disengaged students or unprofessional colleagues. We all need to be willing, at some point, to both have and accept conversations that might make ourselves or the other person uncomfortable. And it's not only about addressing issues that are seen, but it's also about building trust between the people we work with. The ability to have and to positively receive a challenging conversation helps to build this trust.

When speaking about the need for a challenging conversation, some people will do anything to avoid having it, including allowing whatever behavior to continue. However, the lack of these conversations results in consequences for all stakeholders.

- The behavior may continue
- Other educators might notice the behavior and begin to see it as acceptable (after all, it's not being addressed so they may do it as well)
- The educators that don't see it as acceptable will be irritated that it's not addressed

- These differences create an "us vs. them" climate
- The trust between colleagues could be broken
- The behavior is no doubt affecting student learning and/or the students may see the behavior

Challenging conversations also need to occur when there is a question as to why something is being done. For example, the way budget money is spent, or the implementation of a new initiative. There is definitely a level of maturity and respect that comes with being able to approach a colleague and ask them why something is happening. The ability to have these challenging conversations will get people facts instead of gossip, increase trust and transparency, and lessen negativity from a lack of information. Although challenging conversations are difficult to have, it is more difficult to work in an environment where gossip and negativity reign due to the inability to ask questions for information.

This kind of conversation holds everybody accountable. I typically find that most people want challenging conversations to happen when someone they work with is not pulling their own weight or doing what's best for kids. Some people want it to happen, but just not to them. However, if trust is built and the climate and culture support feedback for growth, challenging conversations are more likely to be accepted as what they are...a way for everybody to be working toward the best learning environment possible for kids. Hal Roberts

(@HalLRoberts), speaker and author of *Pirate On!*, has created a formula to represent culture that speaks to this:

what you create - what you
tolerate = culture

So, the ability and willingness to not only have a challenging conversation but to accept the feedback given to the recipient is important in building trust. What does the willingness to have a challenging conversation say?

There is trust between us

I trust that you will understand, process, and employ my feedback and put it to good use.

Likewise, you trust me to give you feedback when you need to improve, along with asking clarifying questions and for additional explanations.

There is transparency between us

I know I can ask you a question when I feel I need more information.

I know that you will promote a positive climate by asking instead of assuming.

You believe in me

That I can change, I can improve, and I can be better, and you're helping me to do that. If I lose my way, you'll help me find it.

I believe you have the potential to grow and be even more amazing.

Challenging conversations are sometimes necessary to support the people around us. Although they are often looked at with a negative connotation, they don't need to be a negative experience. They can be based on a solid relationship, trust, and transparency, and they can result in growth and change for all involved. Moreover, they are necessary to create an environment where everyone feels supported and is working toward what is best for students.

When distrust has been part of a culture, it takes a great deal of time to get back. I know for me, when I have broken someone's trust, it has taken effort, time and consistency to rebuild. Trust is one of the foundational tenets of any relationship and not having it can be detrimental to both the relationship as well as the positive climate and supportive culture we dream of building. We often discuss teachers not trusting administrators, but I've seen it the other way around as well. Generally, I've found that when administration doesn't trust teachers, they insert compliance measures (sometimes labeled as accountability), which starts a vicious cycle of teachers then feeling not trusted, and subsequently not trusting administration to be supportive. Trust needs to go both ways, and not only do we need to work to cultivate it, but we also need to be trustworthy and reliable to sustain it.

Sending Mixed Messages

In our everyday relationships, we maintain trust by matching our actions with our words. If we say we are going to do something, or we have a particular belief, we follow-up those words with actions that support them. Not only is this same concept important in education, but the initiatives that we implement need to support our beliefs as well. If we compare our mission and vision, the district initiatives, our building initiatives, our policies and procedures, or even the unspoken rules, do they support what we say that we value?

For example, there has been a shift to focusing on educator mental health and self-care, which is amazing and necessary. If we're supporting this value, we would see actions like:

- A district review of compliance and accountability measures to remove unnecessary work from educators' plates
- District-wide initiatives to support mindfulness
- Free mental health counseling services
- Mental health days allowed for sick time/more personal days
- Additional support in classrooms

If mixed messages are being sent, the district may say it values self-care and educator mental health, but their actions might include:

- Telling educators they need to practice self-care but not removing anything from their task lists
- A lack of support services for mental health
- Sick days requiring a doctor's note
- A focus on initiatives that add more to educators' plates

In the latter case, the district is saying they value self-care and mental health but not taking actions to support it, which can cause confusion and distrust. The misalignment of information can leave people feeling off-balance, and the discrepancy between what is said and what is done can feel like the district doesn't say what it means, even if the district doesn't perceive their message that way. In general, if we want to cultivate trust, our actions must support our words in order to minimize the chance of a mixed message.

Focus on the All-Important Why

Thanks to Simon Sinek and his focus on the concept of starting with your *why*, there has been a lot of discussion about the power of understanding your purpose. Knowing and explaining the why has become a driver for learning and professional discussions. I truly believe these things about the why:

- Educators need to know their why to be engaged and have buy-in
- While "for the students" is an important (and should be obvious) why, it's not always the only one necessary and sometimes needs to be taken a step further
- How connected you are with your own why determines your engagement (personally or professionally)
- When you help students know their why, it will increase their engagement in school
- When people don't know their why, they sometimes need to be led down the path to finding it

Teachers need a why

One of my favorite videos on the power of why is Know Your Why by Michael Jr. (2017). In the video, he asks a music teacher to sing Amazing Grace, which the music teacher proceeds to do. Then, Michael Jr. gives the music teacher his purpose for singing. He tells him to sing it like he had been shot in the back when he was a kid and his uncle just got out of jail, and that same music teacher launches into such a passionate rendition of Amazing Grace that the crowd is left standing and cheering. Michael Jr. closes the video clip with, "When you know your why your what has more impact because you're walking in and toward your purpose." Knowing our purpose is so powerful that some of us spend our entire lives looking for it. We innately search for reasons why from the time we are little kids- proven by the incessant use of the word when we're toddlers. We understand from early on that the reason for something is what drives it.

In the book The Power of Moments (Heath and Heath, 2017), they compare knowing your why to understanding your purpose, and they define purpose as "the sense that you are contributing to others, that your work has broader meaning." In studies discussed in the book, they found that when people were only passionate about what they did, it did not necessarily equate to higher achievement in their jobs even though they were happy. However, if they knew their purpose or meaning (or why), they were found to be more likely to go above and beyond the expectations of their positions. These results make sense. I know that if a teacher buys into an initiative, they will do everything they can to make it happen. How do you create buy-in? You help people find their why. You show them the purpose, and this has to be one of the cases where the why goes beyond just "it's what's best for kids." They need specifics.

For example:

> "We are beginning trauma-
> informed training and
> implementing social-
> emotional learning
> curriculum into the school
> day to help alleviate some of
> the trauma-related behaviors.

This is better for students
because it will help their
stress levels, allow their
brains to understand that
they do not always need to
be in fight or flight mode,
and will allow them to use
more of their brain to focus
on learning. We feel like
implementing the social-
emotional curriculum will
fill some of the holes that we
are lacking in our social
skills lessons, and will create
a healthier classroom
community."

This seems simple and obvious, but how often do we tell colleagues the purpose of an initiative? Why we are implementing it? I'm not sure I've ever been in a district that has. This example goes beyond what's best for students and gives purpose to the initiative. Teachers want to know how the new initiative is going to provide additional purpose and meaning beyond how they already care for their students. Many times, districts skip the explanation of the why assuming that everyone should understand the purpose and move directly into the *how*. Not only does the why need to be provided, but it will need to be reiterated when things get hard; when the teachers reach the struggling point of the new initiative. There is *no moving on from the why*, there is only adding on the how.

Stating the district's why or purpose behind an initiative is only the first step because, for some teachers, this may still not help them develop their own why. This difference in belief may vary from initiative to initiative dependent on the topic, and vary from person to person dependent on their beliefs. If the district's why doesn't resonate with them, they will need support in finding the reason they would believe in the initiative through thoughtful conversations with administration and other teacher believers and book studies.

When teachers accept the district's why or develop their own, they will attend the necessary professional development even if it's after-hours. They will implement the necessary components into their classroom, and they will tell their fellow teachers about their successes. They may even spend their prep times moving other teachers to get on the bandwagon. They will have complete buy-in. If an initiative hasn't gotten the kind of attention it needs, I would guess that the majority of the time the purpose either hasn't been identified or didn't resonate with the staff.

Students need a why, too

My son (we call him Goose), is incredibly witty, intelligent, and finds school a bore. He came home from school last year and asked me, "Wanna know the dumbest thing I learned in school today, Mom?" I inwardly cringed. I had no idea what to expect as he has the habit of catching me off-guard with his comments. "I learned about imaginary numbers, Mom. IMAGINARY. As in they don't exist. Next, we are going to be learning about unicorns in animal biology. When am I ever going to use this?" I couldn't even argue with him. I have no idea why we teach imaginary numbers, and clearly, he didn't either. Did he do the homework? Yes, two hours of it. Was he irritated by the experience? Yes, I believe he actually liked school a little less, even. I wanted to be able to give him a reason, but the only thing I could think of was that he had to take that class, which was enough meaning for him to finish the class with a good grade but not enough to care about the learning.

More recently, my daughter told me that her math teacher answered a similar question to a lack of real-world application like this: "I understand that you may not use this concept in your everyday life, but doing math like this exercises your brains. Just like your bodies need exercise, this math makes your brain work harder." The answer made me smile. The teacher had at least taken the time to find a purpose that made sense for what seemed like useless math problems. Now, whether that why resonated with the kids or not, I don't know. But, I feel like she at least attempted to give the kids a greater purpose for doing something that felt useless.

Many times, our kids' purpose for finishing work is getting a grade so they can graduate and possibly pursue post-secondary learning, but that purpose excludes any kind of passion or desire to learn. It's the reason students seem so apathetic toward classes, especially in high school. Many times in elementary, they are still excited to learn, particularly about topics they're interested in. But by the time high school rolls around their why shifts from learning to grades, and grades aren't enough of a driver to keep them engaged or interested in learning. They can certainly have good grades and graduation as one of their purposes, but our jobs as teachers are to help them find their meaning, help them find their why, so they can be fully engaged in learning as well. We often complain about students' focus on grades. Is that our fault for failing to teach them to find a purpose for learning?

How focusing on the *why* affects climate and culture

It only stands to reason that if teachers have lost their why for teaching (part of disengagement) or haven't been given a purpose for an initiative, policy or procedure, they will not be 100% invested in what they're doing. And if there's any profession that we need total effort and complete engagement, it is teaching. I have seen teachers who have buy-in throw themselves into supporting a successful initiative. Teachers, especially strong, positive teacher leaders, have so much more influence than they know. When we provide the purpose and reason for what we do, both climate and culture can take a positive turn. On the flip side, if we never provide the purpose for the decisions we make, educators feel disheartened, lost, and professionally distrusted.

Creating the right climate and culture might be the most important components for establishing an environment where innovation and divergent teaching is revered and celebrated. It's imperative for teachers to feel comfortable and supported in their workplace in order for them to be willing to move outside their comfort zone and try a new idea where failure is possible. When teachers experience these kinds of conditions and how it encourages their own learning and growth, they are more likely to implement these same philosophies in their classroom to mimic those same results with their students. Filling the holes in the foundation of climate and culture will support effective leaders in supporting staff and students to move forward.

Chapter 3 Summary

The positive (or negative) relationships you create will determine the climate and culture of your school.

<u>Opportunities to improve climate and culture:</u>

Educator Engagement
When educators have disengaged from their profession, they have forgotten why they got into teaching, to begin with.
Change: Bring attention to teacher disengagement and provide support for mindfulness and mental health.

A Foundation of Trust
Trust is the foundation for building a positive climate and culture. When broken, it takes time and targeted effort to develop. Trust can be broken by action or inaction and can be one cause of disengagement.
Change: Trust takes time and massive amounts of effort to heal. Focusing on rebuilding trust means paying attention to both the messages you say and the messages you unintentionally send, being proactive and sensitive to people's issues, and being reliable.

Opaque Transparency
Transparency tells people why something is happening. Lack of transparency and initiatives will confuse and irritate people. If there is a lack of trust, more transparency is necessary.
Change: Be aware of trust issues in the district and adjust transparency to what people need. If you don't know how much information is necessary, ASK.

Mixed Messages
Do your district initiatives support your values? Do you preach teaching the whole child but focus only on data in literacy and math? Mixed messages leave people feeling overwhelmed and disorientated.
Change: Align your district values to your initiatives, policies, and procedures. If you don't know what the district values are, begin by writing those.

Focusing on the Why
The why gives people their purpose and creates buy-in. Too often, we move directly to the how and ignore the why.
Change: Be explicit and purposeful when giving people the reason for an initiative. If the district's why doesn't help educators find theirs, offer them additional support to find it. Help them find what connects them and creates buy-in.

Chapter 3 Reflection Questions

1. Is risk-taking allowed in your school? Encouraged? What behaviors, practices, or norms tells you it is or isn't?
2. How can the district better support and communicate the idea of risk-taking?
3. What would you say is the level of trust in the district? Among teachers? Between teachers and administrators?
4. List three specific ways that trust could be either continued or rebuilt.
5. What opportunities for improvement do you see in your district?
6. Most important: Would your teachers and administrators answer these questions in the same way?
7. Do you believe you have a voice in your district? How does this affect student learning and your attitude toward innovation divergent teaching?
8. How can you advocate for more voice for stakeholders who may not have as much?

Chapter 4

Effective Leadership

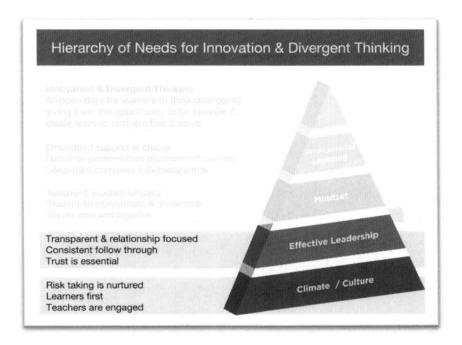

I was once listening to my friend Adam Welcome (@mradamwelcome) speak about leadership, and he said that you can take a great leader and put them on an ineffective team and they will be able to morph that team into effectiveness. The opposite also holds true. If you have an effective team and switch out an effective leader with an ineffective one, that team may fall into ruins. The effectiveness of a leader (or leaders) in an organization can be so influential that a change in leadership can cause a tidal wave throughout the entire organization, either positively or negatively, depending on the actions, values, and established relationships of the leader.

For this reason, and because people can typically relate to the influence that a leader can have one way or another, the switch between climate/culture and effective leadership is by far the most requested change in the hierarchy.

However, I've placed effective leadership above climate and culture for a very specific reason. An already established positive climate and culture will continue to support an effective leader so they can move forward, create change, and support mindset, professional learning, and innovation and divergent teaching.

I believe that an effective leader put in the position of needing to fix a negative climate and build a strong culture from a weak one will be able to do just that. But it will take away from their ability to move an organization forward immediately when they are forced to take time and energy away to fill the holes in the foundation of climate and culture. I also believe that an ineffective leader can be the catalyst for issues in a positive climate and culture.

Inevitably, when I tell people that leadership drives these types of changes, they respond with an off-handed remark about an administrator they worked for who lacked leadership skills. But administration is really a very small percentage of the leadership needed in a district to move it forward. Teacher leaders (as in the teachers who exhibit leadership qualities, not necessarily just the role labeled teacher leader) are crucial components of a successful educational ecosystem. A teacher leader should never underestimate the power they have to create positive change in a building or district because when it comes down to it, these people are some of the main drivers for change. Everybody's strengths are needed to do what's best for student learning. Administration can certainly not do it alone. As an administrator, if I really want change and buy-in for an initiative, I'm going to my strongest teacher leaders and asking for help. I guarantee that the teacher leaders in our schools have so much more influence than I could ever have.

Also, the reason effective leadership includes all leaders (versus just administration) is that the act of leadership is a way of being, a choice. It is not a role. True leaders choose to positively influence others so the people they influence *desire* to move forward. I have been in a district where the superintendent was phenomenal. He was exceedingly kind, people knew he had their backs when it mattered, and when he retired, people were legitimately upset because they understood that his retirement was a huge loss for the educational community. I have also been in a district where the superintendent couldn't remember my name, had no idea who I was, and I only saw her once at the beginning of the year at convocation. One of them, I would have followed anywhere and trusted to make important decisions based on the relationship that he had formed with the district. The other one I didn't know well enough to feel any kind of support. Both of them were in leadership positions, but I'd only consider one a leader.

Qualities of an Effective Leader

While styles and personalities may differ, effective leaders have certain qualities or habits that other people are drawn to. I was reading a post by Peter Economy, best-selling author and known as The Leadership Guy for INC Magazine, called the 10 Powerful Habits of Highly Effective Leaders (2014). This list with descriptions is adapted from that article:

Confident but not arrogant

People are attracted to leaders with confidence. They appear stable and calm during times of duress.

A persuasive communicator

Leaders know the proper message to deliver at the proper time. They understand that sometimes an inspirational message is needed, and at other times a more direct approach is needed.

Sensitive and responsive to others

Having the instinctual ability to read others and understand their needs along with the genuine concern for their wellbeing. Economy says, "Think about the people in your organization and consider yourself a guardian for their well-being and success."

Determined

Had I created this list, this is where I may have replaced determined with relentless. Leaders follow through, they monitor the details while staying focused on the goal, and they're not afraid of failing and trying again.

Supportive

Great leaders are supportive of their employees both personally and professionally. They genuinely care about the happiness and success of their employees.

Distinguished

Leaders are aware of how they are viewed professionally and cultivate their image, leadership style, and brand while still making themselves accessible to their employees and colleagues.

Responsible

Good leaders understand that a team's performance is their responsibility, during times of both positive performance and when the team needs a redirect. Also, knowing the importance of public praise but quiet redirect is important. Economy says, "When you can do this without singling out people for errors, or assigning blame to others to avoid taking responsibility yourself, you're being a responsible leader."

Optimistic

Passionate leaders are those who "enthusiastically dive into most things with calculated recklessness." They bring genuine excitement to the workplace that is contagious.

Honest

Being honest, ethical and taking others into consideration when making decisions is a critical component of effective leadership.

Organized & together

Effective leaders have the ability to plan ahead, see the details, and be forward-thinking. If you're a great leader, you will have a balance of "lead with your head and your heart."

When I think about the best leaders I've worked under, I agree with all of these traits. However, I've also always believed that the education profession is its own beast. Educators need special skills to work in the industry we do. I have added these additional qualities to try to encompass the characteristics an educational leader should have:

Empathetic & compassionate

Good educational leaders can empathize with all stakeholders. They are compassionate, and they understand that everyone has a story and is carrying a burden that most know nothing about.

Models behaviors

Effective educational leaders will model the behavior they desire to see. If they would like more social media interaction and global interaction for teachers, they are taking the time to grow and interact with their own PLN (professional learning network). Modeling behaviors that we ask of others will show them that we find so much value in them that we are willing to make time to do them ourselves. It also eliminates the "do as I say, not as I do" perception, which can negatively affect trust.

Understands appropriate communicative differences

They can effectively move between student and adult interaction. Understanding the difference between communicating with children and communicating with adults is imperative. Once a professional learning leader walks into a session and addresses us with, "hello my little friends" like I'm back in kindergarten, they've lost me.

Truly & authentically reflective

Educational leaders look at a situation through personal reflection; "what could I have done differently for that situation to have changed?" instead of "if so-and-so would have behaved/listened/participated, it would have gone better and would have been successful." They understand that their reaction to every situation can change it and desire to be more proactive going forward.

Recognizes themselves as a servant

Good educational leaders understand that the "higher" they go in a district hierarchy, the more people they serve. When you start to understand that your job is more about lifting people up than it is about holding people in compliance, the lens in which you look at your role shifts.

Recognizes trust as essential

Educational leaders place a high value on trust and know that it goes both ways. They appreciate that for a trusting relationship to happen, they must trust the people they serve in doing their jobs and making decisions as much as they expect the people they serve to trust them.

Supports risk-taking & learning from failure

Supporting someone to take risks moves beyond saying you support risk-taking. There are stages of risk-taking.

1) Choosing to take the risk
2) Calculating the possible outcomes
3) Learning new skills to support a positive outcome
4) Implementation
5) Reflection upon the success
6) Using new information to adjust and retry

Educational leaders support the entire risk-taking process, not only with positive encouragement but also with the necessary skills training and opportunities for collaborative reflection.

Understands perception is reality

One of the most overlooked qualities of an educational leader is the understanding that people's perceptions are their realities. Once leaders have grasped this idea, they will be able to adjust their own communication to best fit other's interpretations and better equipped to handle misinterpretations as they will be able to employ more understanding and empathy.

Recognizing that perception is reality is especially important when considering the qualities of an educational leader and comparing them to your own. Many times, people look at a list of leadership qualities and mentally rate their own administration's abilities. However, these lists would be best used as a point of reflection. Instead of only asking, "How responsible of a leader am I?" one could also ask, "How responsible of a leader am I perceived to be by my colleagues?" The perception of your leadership by others is more important than how you perceive your own leadership qualities because understanding the differences can help you find weaknesses. Our job as educational leaders is not to tell people they're wrong, our job is to shift their perception.

One of the biggest issues I've seen regarding ineffective leadership is when the people placed in leadership roles do not have a true pulse on their organization. If there is a shaky trust between teachers and administration, teachers may not give honest feedback. Therefore, the administration feels like everything is going well and it perpetuates whatever mistrust they have created. From the teacher perspective, they don't believe that they will make a difference anyway, and they choose not to put their positions in jeopardy. It is a Catch-22 and a clear indication of a lack of trust (see the topic of rebuilding trust in the previous chapter).

In the hierarchy, I added the elements "transparent and relationship focused," because these encompass many of the traits listed in the leadership habits. It is difficult, if not impossible, to create authentic relationships and connections if a leader is not empathetic, as well as compassionate, trustworthy, supportive, and sensitive to other's needs. In an authentic connection, a colleague will never wonder if an attempt at a positive interaction was merely because the leader needed something from them. I truly believe that when there is an authentic, positive relationship between a leader and the people they serve, both sides will walk through fire to make certain that they have what each other needs to be successful.

Leadership and the Depth of Relationships

Recently, I was working with the administrative team at a school district near Chicago. We were dissecting the Hierarchy of Needs for Innovation and Divergent Thinking, and like many times during the Hierarchy workshop, we began to talk about relationships. Because relationships are the foundation for so much of what we do in education, it should be the focus of any conversation regarding change, growth, or improvement.

What we often don't get specific enough about is the depth of relationships we have with our colleagues. I've always felt like I wanted to treat the people that I work closest with like family. It was the same way in my classroom. . .my students were like my children. Many times, there is this unspoken uncertainty about how close a leader should get to their colleagues. It's a fact that during the week I spend as much if not more time at work with my department than I do at home with my family. I want to care about these people. I want them to authentically know me. I want people at work to understand that if I ask them how they are doing, I legitimately care about their answer. They need to know that if they are having a bad day, I will stop what I'm doing and listen.

Leaders can become more effective by beginning to truly value the relationships with the people around them, whether we are speaking about the custodians, parents, students, teachers, paraprofessionals, or any of the other multitudes of support systems that we have in place in education. Efficacy also improves when a leader is reflective enough to monitor and evaluate the consistency between their own perception of their leadership and the perception by those they serve.

In a video interview on Inside Quest with Tom Bilyeu (n.d.), Simon Sinek discusses two ways that great leaders separate themselves regarding the depth of relationships they create.

I've got your back

He points out how in the military, they refer to each other as brothers and sisters, and how these kinds of relationships indicate a unique level of closeness. You may bicker and argue things out and tease each other, but if anyone is attacked, they know that they have each other's backs. While I would say that I definitely do not have this kind of relationship with all the teachers in the district (not that I don't want it, but I have yet to get to know them well enough), I do have it with my immediate charges in my department. I have bickered with them, we have disagreed, and I have almost immediately turned around and gone to bat for them if they have been treated unfairly. I am 110% positive that they would do the same for me at all times. I have taken the heat for them when they have made mistakes because at the end of the day, it is my department and I am responsible for what happens there. We have needed to apologize to each other for mistakes we've made, and because of the strength of our relationship, we continue to function effectively, meaningfully, and intentionally. It has been necessary for us to have difficult conversations that have made us extremely uncomfortable. Real relationships are not always smooth and without frustration and irritation.

What else it means is that I trust them to do their jobs and they trust me to do mine — they always know that every decision I make is with their best interests in mind, and if they move forward with one of my decisions it's because they agree. If they didn't, I trust they would tell me. That is the depth of relationship I want with my team.

I have cultivated these relationships by taking the time to get to know each member of my team. I know what makes them tick, know their little eccentricities and strengths and weaknesses. There are times where I support their weaknesses without making them aware because I feel their weaknesses don't need to be constantly highlighted as they are making growth. Sometimes, we all just need support without the reminder of our pitfalls. I have attended funerals, laughed with them until I cried and struggled to breathe. I have been honest about areas where I need professional support as well, and have asked them for it. I am forthcoming about what I don't know, and when I make a mistake, I tell them, and I apologize. Creating these types of relationships isn't rocket science — it's just treating people like they're human and in turn, acting like you are, too.

I will follow you no matter what

For me, the most powerful and inspiring piece from the video came near the end when he said:

> Courage is not some deep,
> internal fortitude. You don't
> dig down deep and find the
> courage. It just doesn't exist.
> Courage is external.

Our courage comes from the support we feel from others. In other words, when you feel that someone has your back, when you know that the day you admit you can't do it someone will be there and say, "I got you. You can do this." That's what gives you the courage to do the difficult thing. . .It's the relationships that we foster.

It's the people around us that love us and care about us and believe in us, and when we have those relationships we will find the courage to do the right thing and when you act with courage, that in turn will inspire those in your organization to also act with courage. . .

Those relationships that we foster over the course of a lifetime will not only make us the leaders that we need to be and hope we can be, but they will often save your life. They'll save you from depression. They'll save you from giving up. They'll save you from any matter of negative feelings about your own capabilities, your own future, when someone just says, "I love you and I will follow you no matter what."

I love you and I will follow you no matter what.

One of my mentors often asks me in regard to anything I take on, "do you want to be good or do you want to be great?" I know that if I want to be a great leader, my focus needs to be on building these kinds of relationships because there is no way that when I leave my position anyone is going to say, "Wow, she was a great leader. Remember how she had us use that Trello board for organization? I'll never forget that. That was amazing." They will remember the way I made them feel, the ways I showed them I cared, and how I always had their backs. I will remember how they gave me the courage to try to be a better leader and teammate, and to pick battles I may not have otherwise picked because of the support I knew I had when I returned to our department.

The amount of growth I experienced when I moved to my administrative position can be credited to the amount of support that I have received directly from the people on my team and my mentors. We all took the time to cultivate those kinds of relationships together and it has made all the difference in the way our department functions and the positive feelings we have toward everything we are able to accomplish together.

When the Going Gets Tough

Consistently exhibiting good leadership qualities is not always easy. When you understand that your behavior should be the model for others (adults and students included), being on point constantly can be draining. Sometimes, I even find myself slipping into thoughts that would not indicate a good leadership mindset. For example, recently when a colleague relentlessly questioned a decision I made with an intensity that would have impressed me had it not been *my decision*, I eventually wanted to tell her, "Please, just do it. Just do what I'm asking and stop asking questions." I wanted to say those words so badly. I was tired, it had been a long day, and I just wanted something, *anything*, accomplished so I could check it off my list. It was absolutely necessary for me to purposefully and with great cognitive effort, keep what I know about good leadership at the forefront of my mind. I needed to run everything I was thinking through several layers of filters prior to it coming out of my mouth. It took effort. Lots and lots of effort.

It is easy to be a leader when everything is going smoothly. It's those times when you're exhausted, you're busy, and when you have people advocating strongly for their own beliefs, that it's effortless to slip into the easiest way to answer people and deal with situations; rely on compliance and "pull the boss card," which is never the right way. Leadership is not always pretty. We often discuss leaders and managers as being opposites, like they're good versus evil, but I don't think that's true. I think there are few times when managing is appropriate.

Often, people that try to lead but exhibit negative qualities are just impersonators. They may look like leaders, they think they know what leadership should look like, they might call themselves leaders (and most likely declare themselves as leaders as often as possible), but they don't know how to fully think like a leader. They have not been given the tools to transform how they react into a supportive, functional, relationship-based, servant leader. And there are definitely ways to tell the difference between a true leader and someone who is adept at impersonating one.

Feedback

When a *leader* responds to feedback, their first thought will revolve around the fact that perception is everything. They will validate the person's feelings, but will ask themselves what they can adjust to change this perception. They will start from within.

When an *impersonator* responds to feedback, they will look for excuses as to why that person feels the way they do. Maybe they will blame outside influences, maybe they will say it's personality issues, maybe they will blame their team. Either way, they will have little to no internal reflection to base their response.

Tone

When a *leader* responds, at any time, the tone of their response will be humble and understanding. They will know that their response will determine the outcome of the situation, and that sincerity must be the foundation of their message.

When an *impersonator* responds, their message will either be sarcastic or defensive. They may give information, but it will be in an, "I don't have time for this," or "I am really above answering this question," manner. They might give you answers that don't make sense because they haven't really heard what you said. No matter the words used, an impersonator leaves behind an air of condescension.

Relationships

A *leader* looks at relationships as the foundation for what all other learning and interactions are based on. They know that spending the time building quality relationships creates the positive climate and robust culture that supports learning.

An *impersonator* values relationships only from the standpoint of when they are valuable. While they might seem to value them during good times, when adversity comes around, the relationships are valued only as much as they are useful.

Support

This one is straight-forward. When you've finished working with a leader, you'll feel lifted up.

When you've finished working with an impersonator, you'll feel pushed down.

Sometimes, it takes experiencing these two different types of leaders to really see the difference. As I've always said, you can learn just as much from someone you do not want to be like as someone you do, but it's so much more rewarding and uplifting of an experience to work with a true leader. And it's not easy to be a leader. There are times when I struggle with what is easy and what is right when situations are hectic, hard, or stressful. I mess up sometimes, and then I apologize. I adjust my course to be better. I just try to be the leader that I would want to have, and learn what I don't want to be from the impersonators I meet.

Influence versus Control

There is a misperception that the amount of influence a leader has comes from how much control they can exert. In other words, you can influence people if you can get them to do what you want by creating a situation where they have no choice, whether they realize that or not. Some people believe that influence is the same as power, and power is gained with compliance measures that people are forced to do.

The fact of the matter is that even with what I know about education and my beliefs about leadership, I will still do what I'm told when it comes to compliance measures because realistically, I want to keep my job. But that's the only reason why. Compliance measures rarely create buy-in. Just because I participate in a compliance measure does not mean the person who implemented that measure has influenced me.

Influencers create change because their passion makes you want to believe what they believe. When I look back on that list, every single characteristic that I have seen in the influencers I know has to do with creating relationships and maintaining those relationships — just treating other people like valuable human beings. The second you forget that we work with other people who have stories, struggles, personalities, quirks, and different strengths and weaknesses, is the second that you have officially missed your mark.

If you start to believe that the amount of power you exert over somebody else is more important than their well-being, you have forgotten why you're in education. I heard a quote from an amazing commencement speech called the *Wisdom of a Third Grade Dropout* by Rick Rigsby (2017) that said, "always make sure your servant's towel is bigger than your ego." Always remembering that legitimate passion and genuine compassion for other people is the way that you change their hearts and then their minds.

Effective Leadership and Innovation and Divergent Teaching

If you've ever wanted to try a new idea, move forward with an innovative teaching strategy, challenge your own assumptions and teach divergently, and you have uttered the words, "I'd rather ask for forgiveness than permission," that is a tell-tale sign that the leadership is not trusted to support the innovative journey. Effective leaders will not only clear a path for others to think and teach divergently, but they will also provide guidance, feedback and ignite more ideas to move people forward.

The leadership of an organization is crucial to its success. The support given by leadership, regardless of whether in an administrative capacity or not, will influence the mindset of the organization and the people in it. Because of the magnitude of difference the leadership can make, it's imperative that effective leaders cultivate other leaders within their organization, and that ineffective leaders are given the support they need to grow and improve.

Chapter 4 Summary

Leadership encompasses anyone who uses their strengths to be the catalyst for change. Leadership can be shown in any role.

According to Peter Economy (2014), effective leaders show these qualities:

- Confident, but not arrogant
- A persuasive communicator
- Sensitive and responsive to others
- Determined
- Supportive
- Distinguished
- Responsible
- Optimistic
- Honest
- Organized and together

I have added additional qualities that I feel an *educational* leader should have:

- Empathetic and compassionate
- Models behaviors
- Understands appropriate communicative differences
- Truly and authentically reflective
- Servant-leader
- Recognizes trust as imperative
- Supports risk-taking and learning from failure
- Understands perception is reality

Leaders cultivate trusting relationships with their colleagues. Sometimes, it takes a great amount of effort to remember how to act like a good leader when situations are difficult. Great leaders create

change by influencing the people around
They understand that control with complia
get things done, but it will never create passionate
followers who love their jobs. Leaders encourage
divergent thinking and teaching.

Chapter 4 Reflection Questions

1) Does your perception of your own strengths and weaknesses match everyone else's reality?

2) How can you work with others to realize their leadership strengths? Weaknesses?

3) How is the leadership perceived overall in your district? Is there a way to improve this perception if necessary?

4) How do you create buy-in amongst the leaders?

5) How do you really feel about risk-taking? Does it differ if it's you taking the risk versus someone else?

Chapter 5

Mindset

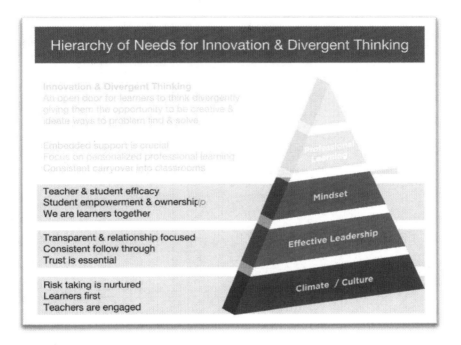

Hierarchy of Needs for Innovation & Divergent Thinking

Innovation & Divergent Thinking
An open door for learners to think divergently giving them the opportunity to be creative & ideate ways to problem find & solve.

Embedded support is crucial
Focus on personalized professional learning
Consistent carryover into classrooms

Teacher & student efficacy
Student empowerment & ownership
We are learners together

Transparent & relationship focused
Consistent follow through
Trust is essential

Risk taking is nurtured
Learners first
Teachers are engaged

Professional Learning

Mindset

Effective Leadership

Climate / Culture

As previously mentioned, when moving between the different foundational levels of the hierarchy, the higher up you go, the more personal of a journey the hierarchy becomes. Mindset is the foundational level where this delineation becomes the most obvious. The reason why mindset can be difficult to change is that although people can be offered information, research, support, they ultimately need to *decide to change their own mindset.* Nobody can do that for them. Therefore, it takes a person with the ability to be genuinely reflective and open to change to shift their mindset.

Many of us are familiar with Carol Dweck's work on growth mindset and understanding that abilities can be developed; they are not set at a certain level without the potential to change. To be sure that we have a common language regarding mindset, Carol Dweck's (n.d.) work describes:

Growth Mindset:

"People believe that their most basic abilities can be developed through dedication and hard work—brains and talent are just the starting point. This view creates a love of learning and a resilience that is essential for great accomplishment. Virtually all great people have had these qualities."

Fixed Mindset: "In a fixed mindset, people believe their basic qualities, like their intelligence or talent, are simply fixed traits. They spend their time documenting their intelligence or talent instead of developing them. They also believe that talent alone creates success—without effort. They're wrong."

George Couros has developed the idea of the *Innovator's Mindset* (2015). Based on the work of

Note:

A false growth mindset or even a fixed mindset is not the same as fundamentally disagreeing with an initiative or change based on data or solid evidence. We can't simply use the excuse of an educator having a fixed or false growth mindset as a reason to ignore their legitimate concern over something new.

Carol Dweck, an innovator's mindset is the belief that abilities, intelligence, and talents are developed leading to the creation of new and better ideas. The innovator's mindset focuses on creativity, creation, and iteration with the idea that failing, reflecting, and growing from that failure is part of the learning process.

Both growth mindset and innovator's mindset work *for* learning. They provide a positive lens for looking at growth and change through development and learning. If we desire a culture of learning, innovation, and divergent thinking, an innovator's mindset should be what we are aiming for.

One area I don't think that we pay enough attention to, however, is the idea of a false growth mindset, which in my mind is the most dangerous mindset of all. A false growth mindset is when a person believes that they possess a growth mindset, but is unwilling to move forward with change because they don't believe it will be effective. I relate it to having an addictive-type behavior. It's difficult to get better if you don't recognize that you have the problem. If you believe that you have mastered the growth mindset but don't actually put it into practice, you may find it difficult to move forward because you believe you're already there. It's difficult to work with a person like this because they are initially excited about a new idea but when implementation comes, they have every excuse as to why it won't work or they can't do it.

So, if mindset change is a personal journey and must be done by the person necessitating the change, how can we support someone in this endeavor? Or how can we go about changing our mindsets if we feel we are the ones who need the change?

Five Strategies for Changing Mindset

1.   Continue to learn

Recognize that we are all continuous learners. Read, be open to new information, collaborate with others, and seek advice from experts. When helping someone else change their mindset, provide them with information, research, and opportunities for additional learning.

2.   Find a mentor

It doesn't matter how long you've been in education, there are people who are smarter and better at your job than you. Find them. Learn from them. I have multiple mentors depending on the realm I am working in. I have a mentor that supports me in my director role and one that supports me in my speaking role, for example. They each provide me with different kinds of support that I need to do my job better. If you're trying to help someone else change their mindset, BE their mentor. Provide the modeling that they need to show them how awesome change can be.

3.   Create goals

Studies like "The Gender Gap and Goal Setting" (Murphy, 2018) show that people who write down specific, meaningful goals are more likely to reach them. We expect students to create goals and work toward them. Shouldn't we do the same? Goals create the feeling that we should be accomplishing the task we set out to do. Incremental changes to meet goals allow us to "practice" thinking about change and growth as a positive opportunity until it becomes more second nature.

4.   Know your weaknesses

I am confident in where I fall on the growth or innovator's mindset continuums. This is less because I think that I have a complete growth mindset or innovator's mindset, but more because I am reflective enough to know where my weaknesses are and to be cognizant of how they affect my reactions. For example, I preach failing forward (learning from our failures and using that knowledge when we try again), but my first reaction to my own failure is sometimes one of dissatisfaction and disgust. However, because I know this about myself, I am able to work through those feelings by using the information I know (failure is a part of the learning process, we can't grow without it) and support myself with that type of thinking instead.

5.   Develop core beliefs & find your voice

When you develop your core beliefs, you have a foundation on which to base every decision you make. When you don't know what you stand for, it's difficult to know if a change or new initiative is something you support or just another change for the sake of change. When you know what you believe, it gives you a platform for moving forward or moving others forward. Core beliefs support your voice. Develop that voice by blogging or participating in reflective journaling of some kind.

Core Beliefs

I often speak of my core beliefs. I even address them in my keynotes. While I believe everyone has core beliefs, I don't know if many people develop them over the course of time by reflecting and actually writing them down. What I find when I speak to people about them is they often have fragmented thoughts put together on what they think they believe. This is a good start but to really have a strong foundation, core beliefs must be more solid and cohesive.

I developed my own beliefs throughout writing my blog and looking for patterns in my thinking. I am positive that for me, deep reflecting needed to come in the form of writing things down. For this kind of reflection and developing your core beliefs, there needs to be some sort of catalog of thinking to connect the patterns, whether it's blogging, journaling, or creating reflective videos. There are many choices for what platform to use, but it's important to choose something that can be reviewed so that common threads can come to light.

I think that when people read a piece from someone they consider to be a "writer," they think that person must have a natural tendency toward writing. It's important to understand that when I began my blog, not only did I feel like I didn't have ideas that anyone else would want to hear, but I also wasn't convinced that I even had much to say. More importantly, I did not consider myself a writer. Not even a little bit. I never found solace in writing poetry when I was younger, I did not write short stories for fun, I never did any of those things that would lead me to believe that I could maintain what I was attempting to do. Like most new attempts at a project, it took practice, failure. It took me actually realizing that I was writing my posts for myself, for my own reflection and ceasing to write for what others might want to hear, for me to become more comfortable with the discomfort of writing. When I grasped that completely, my posts became significantly easier to produce. Because I did not consider myself a writer and never had ambitions to write publicly, I am convinced that anyone can begin the journey of reflection through writing with practice just like I did.

Developing my core beliefs has had a deep impact on my professional practice. I am more steadfast in my decisions because I know the basic tenets of what I believe. I can list them off and give you information as to why I believe them off the top of my head because they have become embedded in who I am as a professional. Developing these beliefs has been one of the best "gifts" I have given to myself. They have occasionally been my lifeline when I am unsure of myself and what I am doing, and they have tethered me to education and students in a more concrete way.

Most importantly, they are mine. They are a direct result of me taking the time to reflect and find what is important to me. While people might agree with my core beliefs, they may have their own for their own reasons, and that is exactly the way it should be.

An Example of My Core Beliefs

For example, one of my core beliefs is: We need to teach people to do the things we ask them to do.

My best example of this is when we ask kids to reflect. If you have children of your own and you've ever told them to go to their room and think about what they've done, you know you walk in ten minutes later to them playing with their Barbies or Legos, most likely completely oblivious to what they were supposed to be doing when they were sent there. They probably sat on their bed for three minutes and rewound the situation in their heads, wondered how long mom or dad would be angry, and then began playing with their toys. At most, they may have thought about how angry they were at their brother/sister for getting them in trouble. They probably did not reason through what they could have done differently to avoid getting into trouble unless you, as a parent, walked them through that process.

The same holds true for our kids in school, no matter the grade level. We often ask them to reflect, whether it's about a goal or assignment, or even their behavior with another student, but we never teach them what that looks like. We rarely give them examples and walk them through role-play situations with an external dialogue of internal thoughts. We don't show them how to avoid beginning reflection with what someone else did or blaming circumstances out of your control, but instead focusing on what role you had in the situation and what you could have done differently to change the scenario. We don't teach them to create a mental plan of how to change the scenario's outcome in the future by making different choices. I am positive that I did not learn how to be truly, deeply reflective until I was about 38 years old, and it was only because I taught myself and practiced, not because I was taught in school.

Many of us who plan professional learning opportunities do this with teachers as well. We say things like, "Use Twitter" or implement a new initiative, but then don't give them the necessary professional development to learn it. We need to provide educators with an abundance of (not only the necessary) professional learning opportunities and follow-up support to do the things we ask them to do with students, as well as to model what we are asking them to do.

This first core belief has spurred me on to finding additional ways we can provide professional development support to teachers. It has made me aware as an administrator, of what I am asking teachers to do and if they need additional help in getting there. It may be in the form of buy-in or developing a new skill set, but I try very hard not to ask if I'm not willing to provide the learning. I have learned to try to not assume, and if I do, to challenge those assumptions. This same idea can be carried over into the classroom. It's one of the reasons that I practiced everything with my students before releasing them to do it on their own. We practiced procedures at the beginning of the year, for example. We role-played, and we worked through reflective practices together. While I hadn't developed my beliefs to this extent at the time, I realized later that this has been an embedded belief even back to my classroom days, and still continues to drive me in my current role.

This core belief (and the reason I believe in it) is an example of the foundation I have built by reflecting. My other core beliefs are as follows:

- *Is this what's best for learners?*
- Mental health support is imperative for educators and students.

- We need to model the behaviors we want to see.
- Start with empathy.
- We need to take responsibility for our own learning.
- We are only as good as the people we surround ourselves with.
- Focus on the *why.*

The first "lesson" of developing core beliefs is to begin to write and reflect, even if that "writing" is jotting down three thoughts a day that you had at some point that seem significant. They don't need to be mind-blowing or deep thoughts. Just three thoughts. You're not necessarily looking for an epiphany, you will develop your beliefs by looking at patterns. Another option: begin a blog. Whether it's public (which I recommend so you're sharing your thoughts and giving back to your PLN) or private, or written or a video blog (vlog), begin to chronicle your journey. The patterns you find after time will help you develop your core beliefs.

I believe that the most important tool we have to change mindset is reflection, and focusing our energies on organizing our thoughts. If our thinking is scattered and chaotic, more energy will be necessary to focus on change and growth. Developing the right mindset to move forward effectively will provide a basis for moving forward when beginning to focus on personalized professional learning.

Analyze your Attitude

In education, many of us say we are agents of change, and everyone needs a growth mindset. I heartily agree with all these things, but it doesn't mean that change is easy, and it also doesn't mean we should claim it is when it's not. I innately stink at change. That probably seems like a strange quality to admit while working in the field of education, especially when my current title clearly has the word "innovation" built right in. I'm not afraid to admit it because I know that I recognize this weakness. I need to be cognizant of the way that I react to it, and I can be reflective enough to adjust the way I react to changes in the way that I would want to model for other people.

I know, however, that the way that I react to change and my attitude toward whatever adjustment I need to make will dictate the way I feel about the resulting difference going forward. How I react will also have a positive or negative effect on the way people around me will feel moving forward.

I was recently in two separate situations where a decision I made about a change was questioned by a colleague. In the first situation, the teacher asked me about the change, and I explained the why behind the decision. Even though she didn't necessarily agree with the outcome, she shrugged her shoulders, thanked me for explaining, and smiled before walking away.

In the second situation, I was approached by a teacher in a hall. He was angry and confrontational, and even though I typically have complete faith in providing the why behind decisions, it was clear that in this case, he was not ready to hear that (hopefully, yet). My attempt at explanations did nothing, and he left the conversation nearly as angry as he came to it. The encounter didn't make either of us feel satisfied or good about the outcome.

Two very different reactions to change.

There are times when new initiatives and change can be extremely difficult, especially when the decisions made feel top-down. We have very little control over what's happening in a profession as personal as teaching, but the one thing we do have complete control in is how we react to change. We can dig our heels in, or we can make the decision to accept the change and figure out a way that we can make it work positively for us. Maybe the change creates a situation where we need to be thinking creatively and innovative inside a box. The change might force us to think of new ways to do something we've done for years, and surprising ourselves by finding an activity or strategy that we wish we would have been doing all along. Maybe it's about revisiting whether the change was actually better for student learning, or if it was just more convenient for us.

I admit change is difficult for me because, at my very soul, I could definitely be one of the teachers needing to be dragged along kicking and screaming for anything new. I need to work hard at accepting it and embracing it because it's not something that comes naturally to me. It's not that I *can't* do it; it's that I need to work really hard to be successful.

Conquering Fear

Fear is a mental game. As quoted in the previously mentioned young adult novel Divergent, "Becoming Fearless isn't the point. That's impossible. It's learning how to control your fear, and how to be free from it, that's the point." Below are four ways to change your mind about fear taken from 4 Mental Tricks to Conquer Fear by Geoffrey James at Inc. (n.d.):

Value Courage Over Security: In facing fear, we tend to side with what makes us feel safe. Replacing the desire for security with valuing courage is one way to deal with fear.

Differentiate Between Fear & Prudence: Possessing some level of prudence is appropriate. Being fearful of driving a motorcycle recklessly, for example, is a good time to practice prudence. However, if a fear is unreasonable and holding you back, like trying an innovative teaching strategy, then you need to push prudence aside and work through the fear.

Treat Fear as a Call to Action: Write a plan to conquer your fear and put it into action now. Creating an actionable plan can help work through your fear and help you gain control.

Reframe Fear into Excitement: Like riding a rollercoaster can cause fear and be simultaneously exciting, taking a fear and reframing it can associate it with something that may be fun.

Knowing that I have the ability to choose the way that I react to change is empowering. I think sometimes we assume saying we don't like change means that we're being difficult or not exhibiting a growth mindset, but

that's not true. We all have our personality quirks, and the problem only arises when you use the dislike of something new as an excuse for poor behavior or digging in your heels. When you take a deep breath, think to yourself, "I can take something positive from this," and move forward, that's when you know you've taken a huge step toward choosing a positive attitude and changing your mindset.

Being a Natural

While a growth mindset would tell us that we can learn and grow in any area we work at and practice, it's obvious that some areas just come naturally to people. Activities in these areas are a bit easier to do with little to no effort. There are areas we are not as natural at either, which is what makes us unique. There are quite a few things that I am not a natural at, such as public speaking, chemistry, running (among others). I like to believe that I have a pretty healthy growth mindset, so it doesn't mean I can't do these things — it just means I need to work much harder to be able to do them well.

Public speaking is a prime example. As a kid, I didn't even talk to people, let alone talk *in front* of people. So, when I went to college I took every public speaking course I could find to conquer that fear. Now, I can speak in public and am often in front of people. I joke and say that I live my entire life outside my comfort zone. I am not a natural public speaker, but I can speak publicly.

While I took enough courses to earn a minor in communications in college, I never did conquer my fear. That is, I did not rid myself of it. Instead, I have learned strategies to manage my fear. It is always there whenever I speak publicly no matter how many times I do it or how prepared I am. People will often say, "If you are afraid, why do you do it?" First, I do it because my desire to make a difference is bigger than my fear. Second, I think being afraid of it is *exactly* a reason to do it. It's definitely not a reason to quit.

Many times, I find that people won't try an innovative idea or challenge themselves to think divergently because they are afraid of what might happen. Their fear keeps them from moving forward. However, if we accept that we may always have fears and adopt strategies to manage the fear instead, we may be able to move forward in ways that we previously thought impossible. I believe we view fear in the wrong way. We think we need to get rid of it and when we are unsuccessful, it stops us from trying new things because we think we can't. But in fact, we need to acknowledge its existence and move forward anyway.

We can choose to use our weaknesses as excuses for why we will never improve, or we can use them as motivation for growth and change. Just because something might not come naturally to us, doesn't mean we can't create our own type of success.

The Mindset of a Divergent Teacher

To really differentiate the mindset of a divergent teacher, it's important to recall the definition from Chapter One:

The ability to recognize our own assumptions, look for limitations, and challenge our own thinking regarding teaching and learning. It's taking an idea and creating new thinking that will facilitate student learning in new, innovative directions for deeper understanding.

It is diverging from the norm, challenging current ideas, looking for a variety of solutions, and a willingness to learn from failure and grow.

A divergent teacher is not afraid to challenge current practices and assumptions to find better solutions. They recognize that fear is natural and something to be controlled (and a challenge in itself) instead of allowing it to hold them back. They are reflective enough to understand what their own assumptions are, and in being aware, don't allow their assumptions to dictate how they approach an issue. A divergent teacher also passes the skills and strategies of divergent thinking onto their students.

Chapter 5 Summary

We can give people support to change their mindset, but ultimately the change resides within them.

Carol Dweck's work:

Growth Mindset: "People believe that their most basic abilities can be developed through dedication and hard work—brains and talent are just the starting point. This view creates a love of learning and a resilience that is essential for great accomplishment. Virtually all great people have had these qualities."

Fixed Mindset: "In a fixed mindset, people believe their basic qualities, like their intelligence or talent, are simply fixed traits. They spend their time documenting their intelligence or talent instead of developing them. They also believe that talent alone creates success—without effort. They're wrong."

George Couros's Innovator's Mindset: the belief that abilities, intelligence, and talents are developed leading to the creation of new and better ideas.

False growth mindset: when a person believes that they possess a growth mindset, but when it comes to change that requires the belief in a change in abilities, is unwilling to move forward because they don't believe it will be effective.

Five Strategies for Changing Mindset
- Continue to learn
- Find a mentor
- Create goals
- Know your weaknesses
- Develop core beliefs and find your voice

Core beliefs: the beliefs about education developed over time through deep reflection on educational practices.
Being aware of the way your brain thinks and the attitudes you carry toward topics can help you find

areas where change is needed. Weaknesses or fear shouldn't be things that hold you back. Instead, recognizing those issues, dealing with them, and moving forward can help lead to a successful change in mindset.

A divergent teacher is not afraid to challenge current practices and assumptions to find better solutions.

Chapter 5 Reflection Questions

1) Growth, innovator's, and fixed mindset are a continuum. Where would you put yourself on these continua?

2) Do you know someone who has a growth mindset? False growth mindset? Fixed mindset? What is it like working with each of these people?

3) What do you think it's like working with you, given your mindset? How does your mindset affect the people around you?

4) People with similar mindsets tend to gravitate together. How can you utilize the group's strengths to try to bring them toward having an innovator's mindset and thinking divergently?

5) Mindset is very personal. You can only try to guide people in changing their mindset — you can't do it for them. What strategies do you think you can introduce to others to help them get started on their journey?

6) How do you combat false growth mindset in yourself? Others?

Chapter 6

Personalized Professional Learning

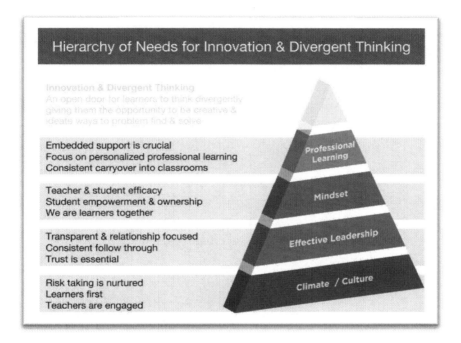

In an effort to support professional learning, personal passions, and to model how we want students to learn, there has been a shift to incorporate personalization into professional learning. However, as I've worked with more districts in many states I've found that in general, professional learning is not given enough consideration in districts. Subsequently, professional learning becomes more sit-and-get in order to jam trainings and new initiatives into a limited amount of time. If we "make time for the things that are important," we perpetuate the idea that professional learning is unimportant by the lack of time we spend on it and opportunities we provide educators. If we say, "we value learning" and then don't embed the necessary time for educators to continue their own professional learning, it creates a disconnect between what we say and what we do. This is one of the most common areas where I find what districts say they value to be lacking in their actions. If we value learning, we make time for *everyone* to learn.

While professional learning is commonly generalized as "professional development," different types of adult learning typically happen in a district. While there is a strong movement toward all personalized professional learning, I believe that there is a time and place for all types of learning. Often, we lump all types into one basket, but not all of it is created equal. There is no silver bullet in student learning, and there is no silver bullet in professional learning, either.

Training

Training is skills-based only learning. It provides opportunities for more efficiency, helps people to have a better workflow, and to understand how things work.

Examples of trainings are:

- How to use Gmail
- Setting up your grade book in your SIS
- Utilizing a new piece of equipment or technology

Professional Development

Professional development helps an educator improve their competence and effectiveness. It provides not only best practices and instructional strategies, but also instills confidence that helps reduce anxiety by providing answers to the question, "Am I doing this right?"

Examples of PD are:

- Setting up/managing a comprehensive reading classroom
- How to implement project-based learning
- The why and how of vetting online resources for learning

Personalized Professional Learning

Personalized professional learning happens when educators choose which of their interests or weaknesses necessitate additional coaching, resources, research, or expert guidance. Personalized professional learning supports educators in their desire to become better teachers. It also allows them to continue to follow their passions while supporting their students in finding theirs.

Examples of Personalized Professional Learning:

- Exploring growth mindset on Twitter and joining a chat
- Connecting via Google Hangouts with PLN members to discuss a book study
- Meeting and collaborating with a technology integrator to learn more about your passion: robotics

Adding Personalization to PD and Skills-Based Learning

While training and professional development are not the same as personalized professional learning, there are still strategies for implementing elements of personalization into training and professional development opportunities to make them more engaging. For example, as a technology integrator, I collaborated with a fellow Google Trainer and integrator, Matt Callahan (@MattCallahan125), on what we called the G Suite Track. We created a course in Canvas (our district's learning management system). Each module within the course was dedicated to one of the main G Suite apps and included skills-based learning, ideas for classroom implementation, an article on technology integration, a discussion board, and an assessment. The instructional portion of the modules had a combination of videos, gifs, written directions, and presentations. Our discussion boards and assessments had three options for activities they could choose to do that were leveled- easy, medium, and difficult (although this information wasn't blatant, we simply asked them to choose one that challenged them). These choices were how we added some personalization to information that would typically be presented in a skills-based learning workshop.

We also provided options to take the course in a variety of modes: entirely online in which they could finish on their own schedule, come to the face-to-face sessions where we taught out of the course (so everyone was getting the same content) but with more support, and a blended option where they could choose from week to week if they would like to attend the session or not. This gave flexibility to those with busy schedules, and it also allowed learners to move more quickly through apps they were more familiar with while taking more time with ones they were not.

While I still wouldn't consider the G Suite Track as being personalized professional learning, it added elements of personalization to training and professional development. It took more time to add these elements to the learning, but it was our best attempt at individualization and personalization of training and professional development. We often miss the opportunity to add these in because time is limited, and we are trying to be as quick and efficient as possible to get the information out.

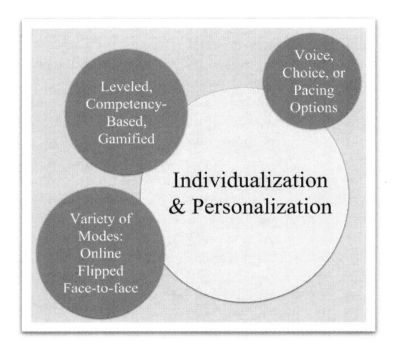

This graphic shows ways that personalization can be added to professional development and skills-based learning.

By continuing the sit-and-get types of training and professional development, we are not modeling the kind of learning that we want students to have in the classroom. I've absolutely been guilty of this myself, but in reality, it is quite difficult to add personalization to any kind of professional development when you're told, "You have 20 minutes. . .go!" If more time was dedicated to purposeful, personalized, and educator-driven professional learning, the growth would have a chance to make it back into the classroom where it would affect students, just like

An important element of personalized professional learning is taking responsibility for our own growth. There are ways to use social media for just-in-time learning for what we need to know. For example:

- Voxer voice messages allow for asynchronous professional book studies
- Twitter hashtags curate tweets on a specific topic for more information, articles, thoughts, as well as the opportunity to find other educators to collaborate
- Facebook groups or pages give educators with similar interests a place to learn and share ideas
- Flipgrid can be used for either personal video reflection or to curate ideas on a topic with the ability to respond to videos with comments

Thinking innovatively about how we can use social media for professional learning will give us opportunities for collaboration and connections we might not have otherwise.

it's meant to do. It takes a mindset shift and priority given to professional learning as an integral part of education and teaching kids for such impacts to be realized. Again, if we say we value learning, we need to dedicate the time that's necessary to be able to dig into what we need to improve our practice; depth over breadth. In our minds, we know this. It doesn't show up as often in practice.

Professional Autonomy

A potential challenge with all professional learning is the engagement of the participants in training and professional development, and the level of empowerment they feel towards their personalized professional learning. The more they are of the mindset that they are able to learn or that their students are able to learn, chances are they will be more likely to implement changes. In Jarod Bormann's book *Professionally Driven: Empower every educator to redefine PD* (2017), he discusses the idea of sustainable autonomy and how we can build and maintain a trusting system where educators are in charge of their own professional learning without compliance measures. He says:

> Many people are familiar
> with the words sustainable
> and sustainability, but I
> think the definition is worth
> mentioning: able to be used
> without being completely
> used up or destroyed. That
> means it's always there, and
> it stems from a natural
> place, not artificially created
> (pg. 90).

In other words, many times in professional learning, we are focusing on the wrong things. Some districts use extrinsic measures to motivate teachers. When that doesn't work, they implement compliance measures, which takes away the autonomy from high-flyers and puts a glass ceiling on their potential. They can see what others in other districts are doing through the glass, but are capped off by the rules. What we should focus on instead is buy-in and cultivating intrinsic motivation, building the *desire to learn*.

If a participant has complete buy-in for learning, they are more likely to implement it as well. There needs to be a significant level of intrinsic motivation for a teacher to try something new, fail, and then tweak it and try it again. This, coupled with the buy-in for what they've learned, can make all the difference in the success of the implementation. Bormann also addresses this in *Professionally Driven*:

> I've sat in with PD planning teams that give out surveys to see what topics teachers want. When the results come in, inevitably the team looks to see which categories got the most votes/comments. However, what happens is they say, "Oh, that topic got 64%, so that's got to be a top priority for everyone." Everyone? There's 36% of the staff that indicated they didn't need it, so now it's a priority for everyone? This is not an effective strategy (pg. 9).

In this case, 36% of the staff has little-to-no buy-in of what they will be learning. While you may pick up a few people who didn't know they would be interested in what you present, you still have a significant number who will ultimately be disengaged from the learning and have very little chance for implementation.

My last two positions, a technology integrator and the Director of Innovation and Technology, have had an element of professional development planning and implementation in the job description. I have absolutely made this same mistake and have watched others do it as well. I think that sometimes as adults we panic when we are in charge of large-scale learning sessions, but if we spoke with a teacher who was creating lessons that applied to only 64% of their class, we would be seriously questioning their professional judgment.

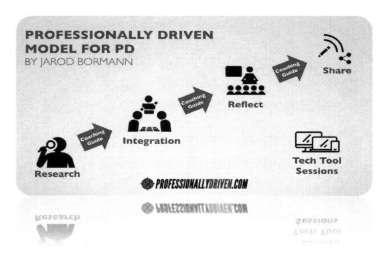

Personalized professional learning: Bormann's model for personalized PD

I have been a part of discussions repeatedly where district administrators say they value learning but undervalue professional learning, or they make the mistake of calling the logistical, housekeeping staff meetings "professional development." I say with 100% certainty that as a teacher, I never left a staff meeting feeling like I was provided with a learning opportunity that made me a better teacher. At some point, I figured out that I was responsible for my own growth, and when I wasn't supported by the district, I found my own support.

I have also been a part of professional learning days where teachers say they value learning but then don't participate in the learning activities presented or take initiative to find their own learning. The effort has to go both ways.

While a professional educator should inherently love learning and be willing to learn from others, they should not be expected to find all of their growth options outside of what the district provides. They should be provided the support they need to grow in the areas they have identified. If they don't know how to identify these areas, they should be taught how to do that as well. Providing these opportunities not only shows educators that we value what they do in the classroom, but that we value who they are as people because we are willing to spend time on them to become the teachers they want to be for their students.

Embedded Support

When it comes to teacher professional learning, I am a true believer in the power of embedded support in the form of effective instructional coaches, given the right culture of professional learning. I feel there are very few implementations that have as large of an effect on teacher follow through and impact on student outcomes. In the most successful coaching scenarios I've seen, the coaches have been content-specific, they have been given opportunities to continue their own learning, their roles have been non-evaluative, and they have resided in cultures where coaching and co-teaching were the norm.

Content specificity

I have worked in districts who have had content/concept-specific positions like literacy, math, behavior, technology, and mindfulness coaches. When we implement instructional coaches, we are recognizing that teachers can't be expected to learn everything on their own and we need experts in those areas to provide support. Sometimes, I will see that a district has hired a content generalist coach. I often feel like this is expecting too much of this coach as well.

We can say all instructional coaches should be focused on pedagogy, but if we want them to be experts in anything, we can't ask them to be a jack-of-all-trades. I know that when I was doing my job well as a technology integrator, I wouldn't have had time to learn what I needed to in the other content areas to do them justice, and I certainly wouldn't have had time to keep up on the newest research. By allowing them to focus on one area, we are telling them to become the best. Again, our goal should be depth over breadth.

Opportunities for continuous learning

Instructional coaches need to be given space to collaborate with each other (across content specified areas) but also in adult learning and the intricacies of coaching such as communication, coaching cycles, and co-teaching. Within the position, there should be an expectation of continued learning and time set aside each week to do so. It should be expected that technology integrators, for example, take time each week to update themselves on new educational technologies because that is a part of how they maintain their expertise. When I was a technology integrator, we would meet as a team with the other content-specific instructional coaches and discuss books and study concepts that were directly related to my position. It was infinitely helpful in understanding how my role was different from a teacher or an administrator.

These opportunities also need to be in the form of ways to connect with other educators outside the district, specifically other instructional coaches. The encouragement to attend conferences, edcamps, and connect online should be part of the professional learning culture. These experiences fuel the fire for many educators. In the case of instructional coaches specifically (since they are responsible for embedded and planned professional learning) it's important that they have the excitement for learning that can be contagious for other teachers.

Non-evaluative

The statement has been posed to me that principals and administrators should be able to be instructional coaches because they should, by the nature of their job, be good resources for effective, engaging pedagogy. While I do believe this to be true, I also believe they shouldn't be the *only* coaches. Instructional coaches should be non-evaluative. It is very difficult for a teacher to be vulnerable, ask for help, fail in front of someone else, and make changes they're not confident in making. It is much more difficult to do that when they believe they are being evaluated. While the nature of an administrator's job says they should be strong in pedagogy and instruction, their position also is inherently evaluative and makes it nearly impossible to be perceived as otherwise, even when they tell the teacher that the visit is just a visit.

Also, even the best administrator has other job duties and functions that will take away from time with classroom teachers. By no fault of their own, they could be called away to deal with a more emergent situation and miss a co-teaching opportunity where the teacher was counting on them for support. This will decrease trust that the administrator will be able to make time for coaching opportunities and diminish the chances that the coaching will happen.

Culture of improvement

There needs to be a common understanding that coaching is for everyone, *not just teachers who are struggling*. Because I live in Wisconsin and the Green Bay Packers have the best quarterback of all time, we often refer to the fact that even Aaron Rodgers (which I'm sure we can all agree is the best quarterback in history) has a quarterback coach. Coaches need to be viewed as 1) someone everyone makes time to work with, and 2) someone everyone needs. Coaches have the unique view of being in multiple classrooms and witnessing the amazingness that is happening across the building. It is the ultimate shared professional practice when we are able to get in each other's rooms. In working with instructional coaches, teachers are able to adjust their own teaching to learn other ways to work with students. Sometimes it's not what they're doing *wrong*, it's what they could do *better*. There's a difference.

Embedded support allows for sharing the responsibility of learning and the addition of collaboration with a colleague who is well-versed in their area. Regarding innovation and divergent thinking, when teachers are able to work with an "expert," it takes some of the responsibility out of learning alone and allows for teachers to focus on what they want to do without being frustrated by how they do it. When the level of frustration is reduced, it enables teachers to feel excited about a new idea instead of anxiety over failure. Co-teaching and coaching cycles give teachers constant feedback and mentoring. And when they fail, it also provides an actual person to help them through the reflection period and to help them find a new iteration of their original idea.

Support for Motivation

I sometimes hear educators refer to other educators as lazy. I believe that word choice can send a powerful message, and in this case, I would change lazy to unmotivated. I feel like lazy implies a fixed quality that can't be changed, while unmotivated suggests that one could be motivated if the right motivation was found. When I look at the teachers who would fall into this category, I mostly (and there are exceptions to every rule) find teachers who are not inherently lazy, but instead people who are disengaged from their profession. I feel like the question here isn't how administrators can force feed motivation into "lazy" teachers, but rather how can we re-engage teachers into their profession? How do we increase intrinsic motivation, so they are the relationship-building, student empowering, collaborative colleagues that would remove the unmotivated label they've been given? What support do they need to become the teachers everyone wants to work with?

We preach student engagement and empowerment. We work toward students taking ownership of their learning, and we want them to be excited to come to school. People say we've taken the creativity out of school, we are teaching to tests, and we focus on facts. We don't give enough time for things like passion projects or allow students to not only find what they're good at but what actually makes them happy. Ironically, we do this same thing to teachers, but then we expect teachers to teach the opposite way from what is modeled for them.

How powerful would it be if we could increase teacher autonomy and relax on the compliance measures for teachers, giving them the opportunity to grow as professionals in the way that they want to? What amazing growth could happen if we would give them opportunities where they take ownership of their teaching and learning, give them the freedom to be creative and divergent in their classroom again, and to eventually be happy and look forward to coming to work?

Some teachers have already done this, sometimes in spite of compliance measures, working innovatively even with the constraints put on them. However, some teachers- just like some students, are going to need additional assistance in finding their voice and being re-engaged in their profession. They need to take ownership, they need to focus on true self-reflection, but they also need support. I would prefer to think of them as having the ability to be motivated, and then work towards a goal like that. A school of professionally driven educators engaged in their craft could have a significantly positive impact on their views of professional learning, innovation, and divergent thinking.

Chapter 6 Chapter Summary

If we believe that learning is important, we will make time for professional learning opportunities.

Types of professional learning:
- Training: skills-based
- Professional development: helps an educator improve their competence and effectiveness
- Personalized professional learning: learning that happens when educators choose which of their passions or weaknesses necessitate additional coaching, resources, research or expert guidance.

Examples of ways to add personalization to training and professional development:
- Leveled, competency-based, gamified
- Allowing for voice, choice or pacing options
- Variety of modes: online, flipped, face-to-face

Professional autonomy shifts the motivation of professional learning from extrinsic to intrinsic. Sustainable autonomy addresses how the environment we create supports or destroys intrinsic motivation.

Embedded support, such as instructional coaches, is vital to a culture of learning. Successful instructional coaching I've seen has had these characteristics:
- Content specificity
- Opportunities for continuous learning
- Non-evaluative roles
- Culture of improvement

Like students, educators have the right to feel empowered in their professional learning.

Chapter 6 Reflection Questions

1) If you had to choose between training, professional development, and personalized professional learning, which would you say is the most commonly offered type of learning for adults in your district?

2) For the training and professional development pieces, are they personalized or individualized in any way? How?

3) How would you like to see the training and professional development pieces changed, if a change is required?

4) What supports are available in your district for personalized professional development? What supports do you take advantage of (i.e., what opportunities do you take for your own learning)?

5) What system do you have in place or can you put in place to guarantee that you are engaged in professional learning that you need?

6) How do you guarantee that you are participating in personalized professional learning that challenges your weaknesses, provides opportunities for growth, and supports your passions?

7) List three ways you can engage in personalized professional learning going forward, including any specific people you could reach out to for support. Who could be your go-tos?

Chapter 7

Innovation Teams

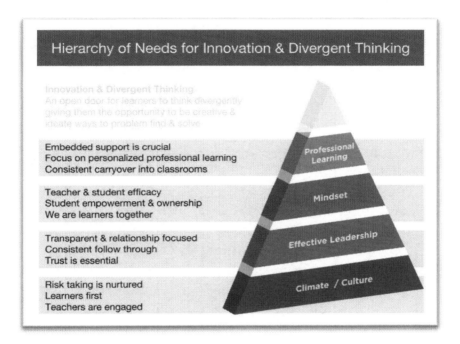

In my role as a technology integrator, I struggled with how to both support and grow the pockets of innovation I saw within the schools where I worked. I noticed educators who were ready to be challenged but didn't know how to ask. I also saw those who showed great potential, but didn't see themselves as innovative and therefore didn't even have the confidence to seek support. I also noted a few who were showing characteristics of divergence. Similar to working with varying abilities in a classroom, I needed to adjust my own practice to meet their needs. The challenge was that they had other responsibilities in their teaching that took up time and they were spread across three different schools. I needed a way to support all these people and grow their capacity in a sustainable, manageable way. From this need, my idea of Innovation Teams was born.

I am a collaborator by nature, so I approached my technology integration team with the idea and my plan. I'd love to say that they jumped out of their chairs and declared me to be the most brilliant of all technology integrators, but that would be a lie. To be honest, it wasn't well-received at all. I was hoping for another integrator and teacher group to move forward with the idea, so we could compare notes and make adjustments, but the support wasn't there. So often, I feel like this is where people stop moving forward with an idea...when they feel like, "my thinking must be (wrong, stupid, off) because I'm the only one who thinks this is a good idea," especially when they have respect for the people who have not been supportive. I could have dumped the idea right then and there. But, I believed I was onto something and was willing to take the risk even if I was the only one to do it. For me, this was diverging from my own norm. I tend to need validation when it comes to new ideas. I was choosing to ignore the fact that I didn't get it and move forward anyway, challenging my own assumption that I couldn't do it on my own. If I ever expected anyone to have faith in me, I had to learn to have faith in myself.

In researching what had been done in the buildings in the past, I discovered that a handful of teachers had participated in what they called "tech teams." The focus in these groups was exactly as one would expect: technology. New devices, new apps, and new rollouts from the district technology department were the primary discussions. But by this time in my integration role, I had come to understand that even though I was called a technology integrator, my role should be primarily focused on pedagogy and innovation. Just being adept at new technologies and apps was the equivalent to being at the lowest level of Bloom's Taxonomy for my position. It was necessary as part of the learning process, but my goal needed to be student content creation, innovative teaching strategies, and divergent thinking and teaching. Therefore, I decided that I didn't want to continue the tech teams because I didn't want there to be any confusion as to what the goals of the innovation teams were going to be. We would focus on the teaching, not on the tech.

TECH TEAMS VS INNOVATION TEAMS

TECH TEAMS	INNOVATION TEAMS
• Focus on technology tools (look at this cool new app!) • Device-focused • What needs to be fixed • Software implementations or pilots	• Focus on learning with technology support • Looks & studies new, innovative approaches to pedagogy • Book studies • Idea sharing, failures & successes

Agents of Change

I began the task of recruiting teams of teachers who I knew had three main personalities regarding innovation and change across my three buildings, although since then I've found these descriptions to be universal.

The Innovators

Actively fight against the status quo. Want to change it up and do what's best for students. Not afraid to fail. Usually excited to share what they do.

The Acceptors

Accepts that everything changes. They might even desire a little change, but aren't motivated enough to look for it on their own. Sometimes may grumble.

The Heel Diggers

Actively fight against any change even if the change is best for students. Usually heavy on the complaints and try to rally others against any change.

I strongly felt that the next few steps in forming the team would set the precedent for how it would move going forward and the level of success that I could expect. I knew that the people who decided not to join the team would be watching to see if it was something they would be interested in, and I was fully expecting to begin a second cohort the following year that would go through all the same steps in learning as the first cohort did. It was critical that I was reflective enough to recognize when my own assumptions about people were getting in my way.

Assumption Challenge #1: While some may look for the innovative spirits only, I looked for all types of people for the Innovative Teams. If I was going to think divergently, I needed to challenge my own assumptions as to *who would be best for the team*. If my end goal was to build capacity, I couldn't look to support only my highest flyers. Honestly, the educators who would create the greatest amount of buy-in to the new ideas would be the ones who didn't subscribe to them in the first place. I needed them to advocate for me. I also had to put aside my own biases for and against people, and to recognize that my feelings toward their personalities had nothing to do with their innovative potential in the classroom.

Assumption Challenge #2: My initial reaction was to limit the number of people who were on the team. My concern was logistical only: I wanted to be certain I could provide quality support to the team members, and I worried about being spread too thin. However, I learned quickly that by allowing everyone on the team, I never had to tell anyone they couldn't be on it, abolishing what would have otherwise been a competition for a more collaborative feel.

Because I recognized these assumptions and was actively fighting against allowing them to put a ceiling on who joined the Innovation Teams, my only requirements for being a part of the first cohort were that participants had to have:

- A growth mindset
- Strong classroom management and the ability to create strong relationships with students
- Dedication to teaching and learning
- A willingness to try new things and fail
- An open mind and to think reflectively
- Willingness to facilitate students
- Resilience and grit
- The ability and desire to empower students
- Excitement at the prospect of transforming the classroom

It's important to note that the mention of even a general tech-savviness was not a part of the conversation. *My* job was a technology integrator and to be tech-savvy. I was confident that I could teach them what they needed in the arena of the technology skills necessary to integrate it into their lessons. However, it would be more difficult to teach someone who did not have the desire to learn or was unwilling to try new adventures.

In reflection at the end of the year, my one mistake with the Innovation Teams was not insisting on the participation of the building administrators and the other instructional coaches. Many times, the math and literacy instructional coaches believed that the technology integrators really had nothing to do with their roles in supporting teachers. I couldn't have disagreed with them more. In my view, the technology integrators should have been a part of every single coaching session because it was their job to understand the pedagogical expectations and intervention strategies of the literacy and math coaches as much as it was the literacy and math coaches' jobs to understand technology integration, innovation and how it supported the learning process. It is nearly impossible to grow as a whole when we are working in silos.

The Pitch

"Help me, help you. Help *me*, help *you*."

In the opening of the pitch given to teachers during their respective faculty meetings, I used the famous Jerry Maguire (Crowe, 1996) scene where Tom Cruise begs Cuba Gooding Jr. to open himself up to new ways of thinking in order to become a football player that teams would want. Only the other instructional coaches gave me a chuckle. I wanted the teachers to allow me to support them. I needed them to know that I desperately wanted to work with them. By this time, I felt like I had a solid relationship with many of the teachers. It was obvious that the ones I worked with the most already had the highest interest and trust in what we could accomplish when we worked together. Their smiles and nods gave me the courage to continue when my attempt at humor with the movie clip was met with silence and had clearly bombed.

I moved through the rest of the presentation explaining the types of teachers I was looking for, introducing what the district had established for their personalized learning definition, what I promised to do for them and what I would be expecting. I was explicit in describing the level of commitment I expected of the group, and how it would match the level of commitment I promised them in return.

As for what we would be doing, the teachers were shown a slide deck with these activities:

- Book study group on *The Innovator's Mindset* by George Couros
- Placing the classroom needs up on GoFundMe to try for some flexible seating options

- Looking at the physical classroom environment and what works best for learners
- Discussing student voice and choice regarding learning and assessments
- Allowing more time for innovative projects for the students by giving them additional support
- Studying personalized learning and what that looks like in the classroom
- And so much more!

I knew I was expecting a lot from people that I could not provide extra pay to be a part of the team. I didn't have that kind of power as a technology integrator. I promised that meetings would be held during contracted hours after school. I asked that meeting times be held as sacred as possible and what we studied would be implemented in the classroom. To be honest, I wasn't sure we would get through everything I had planned. I hadn't started right at the beginning of the year, and I was quickly losing time with the teachers. Luckily, I had underestimated the group that signed up and what they would be willing to accomplish in a short period of time.

"Looking for rockstar teachers!" was what I saw in an email from Mandy and I was instantly hooked! I joined the innovation team and my mindset completely changed. I didn't expect to gain so much knowledge and interest from a simple email.

Innovative teaching completely shifted the way I taught. It opened the door and gave students a choice and voice in their learning. It gave my students flexibility in learning because they felt that they had a purpose; a purpose for learning. Innovation has changed the way I assess students on their learning as well. I've never had so many students begging me to give them their end of the unit assessment! By being on the innovative team, my students smiled with confidence when faced with a challenge.

- Zong Vang, Innovation Team Member

The Innovation Teams

Although I was the technology integrator for three schools, I decided to have one innovation team try to bridge what was happening across the district. For each meeting, I would try to switch schools and hold the meeting for the other two via Google Hangouts, so we were all together. It wasn't ideal, but it worked. I wasn't always able to rotate being at each school as I worked on a flexible schedule and was sometimes leaving meetings too close to make it anywhere else, but I did the best I could.

Roughly 10% of the teachers at each school voluntarily agreed to be on the Innovation Team. Some of them I recruited because I knew they would be amazing. One teacher in particular that I sought out was very vocal about his lack of knowledge in the technology arena. But, he also regularly invited me into his classroom and listened intently to everything I said. He needed more assistance and skills-based learning than some of the other staff, but his desire to learn was second to none. He wanted to know so badly. I approached him not only for his yearning for learning, but also because he loved his students and was a master at forming relationships. Inviting him to be on the team was a no-brainer, but also his invitation proved that I was not necessarily looking for technology literate people. I was convinced I could teach them that. I needed people *ready to learn*.

Phase one

We began with two activities simultaneously: a book study with George Couros's book *Innovator's Mindset* (2015) and studying our school district's definition of personalized learning. I chose Innovator's Mindset for a few reasons. I had facilitated book studies with it multiple times. Each time, I watched it completely transform the way educators and pre-service teachers thought about teaching and learning. Also, I credit George Couros with being a major part of pulling me back into teaching when I thought about leaving the field. I wanted to give my teachers that same inspiration to take back to their classroom.

We studied the district's definition of personalized learning and discussed ways to implement voice, choice and pacing options into their K-5 classrooms. We began with one of the easiest ways to provide choice and worked on developing rubrics based on standards that could be used to assess any type of way that a student would want to show their learning. We also discussed the logistics of personalizing learning, such as the challenges, management, and how to teach kids to effectively make choices (as it's not an inherent skill).

As we finished up the book study, we focused on using social media for professional learning because I wanted them to build a professional network they would be able to reach out to if I wasn't available. My goal was to set them up to be successful without me. In my experience with asking teachers to use Twitter, they need to see two things: 1) that I use it and 2) how it will work quickly and practically for them. While I believe that cultivating relationships within a PLN is the greatest reason to be active on social media, for some people who don't yet have this, they don't know what they need until they need it. Therefore, they look at a PLN as just "more friends" and may not see the value of that support. Instead, they initially need to be shown practical ways to find information that they can use right away — for example, hashtags that will lead them to immediate new ideas and articles or chats where the tweets will resonate with them. I also have an example of how using Twitter and growing my PLN gave me the resources to complete a large project I was working on. This practical knowledge will get educators on Twitter. The relationships they form will keep them there.

And finally, in phase one, we dove into flexible learning spaces. This was actually a strategic move on my part. It served two purposes. First, my experience and research told me that the improvement in student behavior that can be seen in the implementation of flexible learning spaces is nearly immediate and significant. Second, being I had been an elementary teacher as well, I understand that they typically put a great deal of effort into the look, feel, and environment of their classrooms. I knew beginning with a change that would show immediate results in both of these areas would create buy-in to the process and subsequently to the teams. We studied the research on flexible seating and learning spaces, and we made lists of purposes for change and furniture that would fit the needs for each teacher. A few teachers went to their classrooms and asked their students to design their new classroom system. Others took more control and redesigned on their own. Some made incremental changes over time and others took literally everything out of their classrooms and started from scratch. It was their choice how quickly they implemented the group's ideas. To fund the spaces, we crafted a common message and put each of the classrooms on GoFundMe (if you choose to do this, first check with your district's policies).

One of the teachers who completely subscribed to the flexible learning environment idea decided to remove all of her desks. When the custodian became irritated that desks were being removed and the room was difficult to clean, the building administrator explained that the learning environment for students needed to be more important than how easy it was to sweep. Therefore, she was allowed to continue on her quest to redesign her classroom.

When she was finished, the students were in awe. They loved the new places to sit, and they still had their own cubbies and places they could put their supplies. However, not long after spending a weekend on the redesign, she had a few parents email her explaining that they wanted their students in desks and were unhappy with the change in the room. The teacher messaged me upset. She had been able to fundraise quite a bit of money for her classroom and had spent it all purposefully. She felt like all her hard work was causing issues, yet she had already seen a nearly immediate marked improvement in students' behavior.

There are very few times I have tried something innovative and haven't run into some sort of adversity. There have been even fewer times where I have thought divergently, and I haven't been told that it was a bad idea. This is where creating and maintaining a professional learning network becomes very important. These are the people who will support you when you feel like everyone else is against you. They are who you call upon when you need guidance and reassurance.

My advice in this situation was to move a few desks back in the room. I felt like if the students didn't want to sit in the desks, they would eventually ask their parents to be able to sit where they were comfortable like the rest of the class could. In this case, I was right. Within a short time, the parents emailed the teacher and told her their students could participate in the flexible seating arrangements. It was a win on many levels — the teacher didn't need to change much about her original plan, the students got what they needed, and the parents didn't feel like they needed to argue to get their kids sitting in a specific spot. In the end, she decided to keep the four desks anyway as additional workspaces.

Phase One was about creating some commonality in what we all knew —building a foundation. In order to move into Phase Two, which was more personalized, we needed to have a common thread binding us together. The topics we covered gave us a group of people that we could go to with questions or challenges with the implementation of personalized learning, an innovative mindset, and flexible learning spaces.

Phase two

During Phase Two, we continued to learn together but branched out more into topics that were of interest. I continued to try to get into as many classrooms as possible to co-teach and support. During meetings I would introduce a new innovative approach, we would discuss it, I would give a suggestion for some readings or a book, and then we would continue more in-depth discussions individually if it was something they wanted to pursue.

Examples of approaches or ideas we studied were:

- Student Led Edcamps (SLedCamp): adjusting the idea of the professional edcamp, we created an opportunity for students to learn or lead a topic that they were both passionate about and which taught a skill or introduced an idea
- Design Thinking: We used *Launch* by A.J. Juliani and John Spencer (2016) to guide our learning and implementation
- Genius Hour: Pure Genius by Don Wettrick (2017) was suggested, even though his book focuses on the secondary level, we were easily able to adjust for elementary

An endorsement by a fifth-grade student for SLedCamp:
Student Led Edcamp

The beauty of working with teachers across the district who were not in constant contact was that we occasionally had a teacher who was questioning their students' ability to handle a new learning experience, and they would, in turn, hear from a teacher at the same level who had already tried it. One of my biggest surprises from the experience was the depth of collaboration due to the cross-district connections. Although I always acknowledged how different each building was, it never dawned on me that the teachers would have so much to share with each other even though they were in the same district. Because I worked with these people on a regular basis, I sometimes forgot how little interaction they had between grade levels at different buildings. The cross-building collaboration was valuable.

The yearly wrap up of the Innovation Teams included a meeting where we reflected on the effectiveness and logistics of our time together. As I previously mentioned, I was unable to pay the teachers for their additional work, so I kept the meetings to after school and only during contracted time. Their one complaint was that the meetings were too far between and they wanted longer meetings regardless if it was outside of the contracted day or not. I was floored. While I believed that the team was successful, the fact that they wanted more (unpaid) time with me and were engaged in learning more of what we had studied was beyond my expectations. For the following year, I had a list of teachers who wanted to join a new cohort because they watched the amazing growth and innovation the first team had shown.

The Innovation Teams were a subset of how the support for teachers in a district moving toward innovation and divergent thinking could look. Creating a culture where professional learning is valued and supported, leadership to guide teachers and provide consistent feedback, the mindset for growth, and opportunities for educators to engage in their professional learning provided these teachers the structure they needed to learn new strategies, challenge their assumptions, and improve their teaching while building excitement for their own growth and interest areas. Remember, filling the holes in the foundational levels of the hierarchy isn't about how we can force teachers to be more innovative and divergent. It's about how we can support and provide them with the structure to build the intrinsic motivation to want to do it.

Chapter 7 Summary

Innovation Teams:

- Focus on learning with technology support
- Looks at and studies new, innovative approaches to pedagogy
- Book studies
- Idea sharing, failures, and successes

Tech Teams:

- Focus on technology tools (look at this cool new app!)
- Device focused
- What needs to be fixed
- Software implementations or pilots

Innovation Team members needed to be agents of change and had to meet the following requirements to be a part of the team:

- A growth mindset
- Strong classroom management and the ability to create strong relationships with students
- Dedication to teaching and learning
- A willingness to try new things and fail
- An open mind and to think reflectively

- Willingness to facilitate students
- Resilience and grit
- The ability and desire to empower students
- Excitement at the prospect of transforming the classroom

Being technology savvy was not a part of the description.

Phase one:

Book study on George Couros's *Innovator's Mindset* (2015)
Personalized learning definition and standards-based rubrics to allow for choice in assessment
Social media for professional learning
Flexible learning spaces

Phase two:

Consistent co-teaching
The study of new innovative teaching strategies/approaches - teacher's chose focus
Student-led Edcamps
Design Thinking
Genius Hour

Chapter 7 Reflection Questions

1) How would you implement a team that followed the structure of the Innovation Teams?
2) What changes would you make to adapt the team to your needs?
3) List three ways the team could support you and your colleagues.
4) List two potential challenges with the Innovation Teams.
5) List two potential solutions for each challenge.
6) What is something you learned from this chapter that you can implement tomorrow?

Chapter 8

The Peak of the Hierarchy

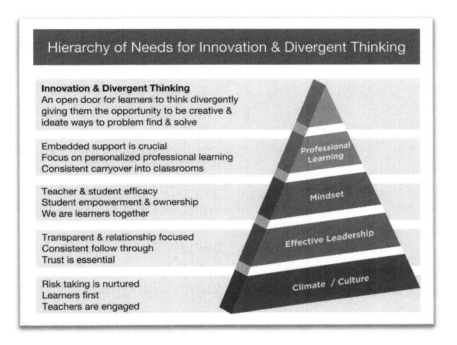

The purpose of the Hierarchy of Needs for Innovation and Divergent Thinking is to give a more concrete look at what supports need to be in place for educators to have the best chance at thinking innovatively and divergently. In looking at an organization realistically, reflecting on these particular support systems is probably going to be more about plugging the holes that might exist in the foundational levels rather than creating them from scratch. For example, you may have teachers who already have a growth or innovator's mindset, but you also may need to "patch" the areas where educators still fall closer to fixed on the mindset continuum by working with them on recognizing growth mindset and swinging their pendulum in that direction. While the idea of the hierarchy should help districts put the supports in place, it still does not "create" innovative, divergent thinkers and educators. Instead, it gives the base supports, so educators can focus on new learning, thinking, and doing rather than using brain space for worrying about other issues around them.

The act of becoming innovative is not something you can be forced to do, nor is it something someone can give you. It is a personal choice to move outside your comfort zone and try to learn something new. Again, even with the Hierarchy complete and solid, that is only the support structure. A person still needs to make the decision to want to be innovative.

Innovation can be messy

As we move toward more innovative approaches, we need to learn, relearn, fail, try again, and use our knowledge to develop new thinking. Rarely is true innovation a straight line to the end, and even when we get to the end, are we really done? Once an innovation continues to be used, doesn't it just become part of the status quo? So, we need to continue the process of moving forward with innovation in order to not become stagnant.

Innovation is personal

I grabbed onto this idea from George Couros. Innovation is personal to each individual. What is innovative to one person may not be innovative to another who has already been doing it, and that is ok. Everyone is on their own personal learning journey. Also, innovation is not an either/or. The idea of innovating and thinking divergently is a continuum, and each person falls somewhere on that continuum. That's why when looking at the people around you, it's best to try to discover what you can learn from each person and how they think differently from you versus trying to compare the amazing things you to do the amazing things they do.

Innovation involves failing

The quicker you accept that failure is going to happen and you will grow from what you learn, the quicker you'll begin your journey. Failing is not always easy, it's not always fun, and sometimes you just want an idea to work. All of that is understandable. However, if the fear of failure stops someone from moving forward and trying again, then that's where the problem lies. Our failures teach us what doesn't work. They are valuable and help us figure out what might work when we try again. That kind of learning cannot be replicated by constant success all the time.

Divergent teaching will stem from divergent thinking

Divergence is the act of thinking and doing outside the box, moving outside your comfort zone, acknowledging and challenging assumptions, being forward-thinking, and using known and recognizing/learning unknown information in decision-making. Divergent teaching uses divergent thinking in all aspects of teaching —from lesson planning to the moments working directly with kids. A teacher thinking divergently will try a new idea with their students instead of scrapping it because they wonder if they can handle it (assuming and forward-thinking). They will actively seek out new information on their own and won't wait for the district to provide all their professional learning. They will allow students to try a new technology that they don't know themselves because they trust their students will learn to use it without their help (recognizing unknown information in decision-making). They will be willing to make quick trajectory changes when they know it will be better for student learning even if the change goes against what they would typically do.

When the hierarchy is in place, this gives educators the chance to move toward this kind of thinking and teaching. If they are worried about what their leadership will say if they fail (holes in climate/culture and effective leadership), they are less likely to try the new idea they had. They are less able to expend energy in bettering themselves as professionals because they are too busy being concerned with the holes in their foundation. Providing people with the support they need in the foundational areas is imperative when expecting them to be innovative and divergent teachers.

Constant Work in Progress

The hierarchy is not something that can be put to rest when the holes are filled. It is a structure designed to support organizations to be constantly cognizant of issues that can come up with changes in staff, leadership, and even student population. One hole can create a host of issues at other levels. A change in leadership, for example, can create a domino effect throughout many foundations of the hierarchy, just as a change in leadership might be just what the organization needs to fill some of their holes. The hierarchy is not a finished product, but rather a constant work in progress, similar to the way innovative and divergent thinking is never truly complete. We will always need to continuously improve to move forward, and that kind of innovation and divergence comes from our own motivation to be the best people we can for our students.

Because the hierarchy is not a one-time implementation, there need to be procedures put in place to create a common understanding among staff that it is a priority. Also, because new staff can disrupt the foundational levels (in good and not good ways), what will be put in place to support them in adopting and implementing the hierarchy? How do we communicate that our values and goals to support innovation and divergent thinking and teaching are not optional, but something that's understood as being a part of the district's culture?

In this way, the hierarchy aligns nicely with continuous improvement. As with implementing continuous improvement, there should be opportunities for constant reflection and revision to practices. In this case, the revisions answer the question: *How can we best support educators in their journey toward innovation and divergent thinking?* This doesn't only mean teachers but administrators, too. If we are following the hierarchy, we know that administrators and leaders must be willing to model what they want to see, and they must feel support in their own journey of innovation and divergent thinking.

Where do we Start?

Issues at the foundational levels of the hierarchy are organizational weaknesses that require individual responsibility. In other words, for any educator to feel like the district is supporting them, they must be willing to take responsibility for their part in both the problem and the solution.

The reason that I call the hierarchy an organizational structure is because every organization is going to have different issues to address, and strengths to celebrate. I've seen districts where building-level issues are specific and are different than the overall district's issues. Also, there is so much more to each of the foundational levels than I could ever address in one book. There are a variety of books whose entire premise lies at just one of the foundational levels.

The first step in applying the structure is to look for common holes in the foundational levels and address them head-on. It would be appropriate to form a team where all buildings and roles were represented (including administrators, teachers, custodians, secretaries, para-professionals, etc.). The people on this team must have the ability to have difficult conversations and the willingness to promote change. There must be a common understanding that the committee's purpose is to develop solutions, not solely discuss issues.

Implementing the hierarchy will be more challenging if only one group or role is deciding on changes that need to be made. For example, if only administration or only teachers decide what the issues are in the foundational levels, will they be able to look unbiasedly at issues from all angles? Are they going to be able to see how certain initiatives are being perceived? *Do they really know and understand what all other roles need to be successful if they are not currently in the role themselves?*

The first place to begin to find and make changes is through the reflective questions at the end of each chapter as well as considering the common issues seen in some of the foundational levels. There needs to be more than surface reflection — digging deep and being completely honest with yourself in what you need to change, and then being willing to have respectful,

professional,   solution-finding,   challenging
conversations.

Climate/Culture

Climate and culture are two of the areas that not only need to be viewed from a district level, but from a building level as well. In moving from a teacher role to a district-level role, one thing I noticed was how easy it was to make that one building your whole world. This makes it more difficult to take an interest in what is happening at the district level because you're living at the building level. There's nothing wrong with this. If we want buy-in to the process, the change needs to be seen at home, too.

Have a team address climate and culture issues by first listing what common ones exist. For example, an issue might be trust. Some buildings I've been in would have said, "mistrust of leadership"; however, if there is a lack of trust for leadership, you can often find a lack of trust within groups of teachers as well. Make a list of norms for behavior and problem-solving as a staff. Think of normal activities for which you wish you had procedures. Sometimes we assume that adults should be able to problem-solve so we don't address how it should be done, but I don't think that's necessarily true for everyone. Creating common understanding levels the playing field for everyone.

Even though climate and culture are building and organizational concepts, everyone within those areas has the individual responsibility for how they contribute to them. If you want to have a place where you feel comfortable, supported, and happy at work, you must want it. You must be willing to make changes. And in some cases, you must be willing to give people a clean slate to see how you can both grow together.

Don't make the mistake of believing that climate and culture changes will be quick. It takes time to change people's perceptions, to support those who have disengaged, and especially to build trust again. If climate and culture are a large part of the issue, be ready to apply an intense amount of grit and perseverance as the work on climate and culture can feel like one step forward and two steps back. While it is often the most difficult, it is also one of the most rewarding foundational levels when you get it right because it supports everything else in the hierarchy.

Effective leadership

The hierarchy is made for leaders (administrators and teachers) to make changes in their own leadership and support the people around them. The leadership in a district and a building are so important that they can make or break this process. If a leader continually defaults to compliance instead of support, it will be difficult for the people around them to try new ideas and think divergently when they're using all their energy to be compliant.

It's important for leaders to have support in the form of a professional learning network (PLN) and also a mentor. It doesn't matter how long you've been in education, PLNs and mentors have the ability to see a problem from the outside and provide guidance you may not have considered. When I have gotten frustrated, these connections have reminded me more often than I'd like to admit that I serve teachers, my department, and students; I am not the compliance police. To grow a network, a leader must be willing to put themselves outside of their comfort zone. They must be willing to have people that not only agree with them, but challenge them as well. There is little value in maintaining a "yes man" exclusive PLN.

One of our most important roles as a leader is building the leadership capacity of the people around us. Recognizing and promoting the strengths of others will build people up and make them more confident to take on leadership roles in other areas. An effective leader alone can make great changes, but a team of effective leaders with varying strengths could be transformational and unstoppable.

Mindset

Again, the foundational level of mindset is where the hierarchy becomes more personal. As stated previously, we can give people all the information on mindset and how to change it, but they are the ones that actually need to make that leap.

The first step in changing mindset is giving people the information they need about what mindset is and providing them with opportunities for reflective activities to evaluate their own mindset. Where do they stand when it comes to change? How do they feel when another colleague, student or parent challenges them? Do they look at innovation as something that should be ingrained in what we do or is it an extra they don't have time for? Do they celebrate the innovations of students or get nervous because the student thought more out of the box than they did? If a colleague comes up with a new idea, how nervous does that make them?

As I described before, my default when I know change is coming is to brace against it because I know I generally don't like it. Understanding this about myself is as important as if I simply embraced change, because when I know it, I can do something about it. Having a growth or innovator's mindset isn't about perpetually being confident in everything you do or not having fears. It's about how you handle those issues when you know you need to move forward. Being able to develop strategies for moving forward when you're afraid or unsure and doing it anyway, that's the beginning of being a divergent teacher. Divergent teachers have many of the same fears that other teachers have, but they have learned to acknowledge that fear and put it in the corner in favor of the amazing things that might happen.

Personalized professional learning

There are three pieces to personalized professional learning: the logistics, the support, and the engagement. Logistically, if learning is considered important, then we need to make time for regular, personalized professional learning opportunities. It can be done. Schedules need to be changed, and calendars need to be looked at through the lens of innovation. Contact other districts to see how they do it. Lengthen the student day and play with an early release on Fridays to dedicate the extra time for professional learning. If someone says it can't be done, I taught in a district that did just that. Some districts are successfully devoting time to professional learning.

Administrative support for personalized professional learning is imperative and includes keeping the time free from other distractions or meetings. The time set aside for learning should not be used to schedule an IEP or department meeting (unless they're the support for the learning).

Embedded support is also crucial. However, there are other ways to provide more support than teachers may have had in the past. For example, create a buddy system for teachers to support each other in their learning journeys. Bring in substitutes every couple of weeks so they can co-teach and support each other during the lesson or the implementation of their ideas (if appropriate). Help them connect with experts and build their own professional learning networks, so they have other people to rely on. How can we build sustainable autonomy? What services can we provide to teachers to build intrinsic motivation and help them *want to be there*? When was the last time they were asked what they wanted and given the chance to choose?

The opportunity for innovative and divergent thinking

When the holes in the foundational levels are filled, all educators will be given the support needed for thinking innovatively and divergently. Everything that accompanies innovation and divergence should be recognized as the way business is done. When the supports are in place, it gives educators the brain space to stop worrying about the issues that are a result of the holes in the foundation; it allows them more time to pursue passions and try solutions that lead to something new and better. Part of building this into a culture is recognizing that everyone is on their own journey of innovation and brings a variety of strengths and interests to the table. As long as they're moving forward, there will be continued support.

Sometimes in education, I feel like we try to answer the right issue with the wrong question. In this case, if our issue is that we desire educators who feel more comfortable taking risks, implementing innovative lessons, and thinking divergently, asking the question, "how can we make people be innovative?" is the wrong one. Instead, the hierarchy addresses what the question should really be: "what can we do to provide educators with the brain space and opportunities to be the people they desire to be?" In completing the foundation levels of the hierarchy, we are developing an environment where the pieces are in place for this to happen.

Chapter 8 Chapter Summary

When the holes are filled at the foundational levels of the hierarchy structure, it allows educators to have the best chance at being successful in innovative efforts. It does not, however, guarantee that. They still need to choose to take that path.

Innovation is a personal journey and not something you can be forced into doing. It's messy, and failure needs to be accepted as part of the learning process.

Divergence is the act of thinking and doing outside the box, moving outside your comfort zone, acknowledging and challenging assumptions, being forward-thinking, and using known and recognizing/learning unknown information in decision-making.

The hierarchy is a constant work in progress and must be revisited often to determine the stability in the levels. To begin making changes, look for holes at each foundational level. Create a plan to fill the holes.

Chapter 8 Reflection Questions

1) The book discusses a definition of innovation and divergent thinking. What would your definition be? Would your definition be the same as you feel your district would define it?

2) Who in your district, do you feel is responsible for setting the tone regarding innovation and divergent thinking? Are they successful? Why or why not?

3) Where are you on your journey? Where do you want to go? Who can help you get there? List three goals that you feel would make you more innovative or a more divergent thinker and the names of people who can support you on your journey.

4) Think about the people you work with on a daily basis. How can you lift them up if they are not as far on their journey as you are?

5) Where can you begin tomorrow? Write down three short-term action steps for moving forward.

References

Administration for Children and Families. (n.d.). Secondary Traumatic Stress. Retrieved May 21, 2018, from https://www.acf.hhs.gov/trauma-toolkit/secondary-traumatic-stress

Bilyeu, T. (n.d.). Retrieved August 26, 2018, from https://youtu.be/TopBJ7fAIgE

Bormann, J. (2017). *Professionally Driven: Empower every educator to redefine PD*. New Berlin, WI: Bretzmann Group.

Bourg Carter, S., Psy.D. (2012, May 6). Where Do You Fall on the Burnout Continuum? Retrieved August 25, 2018, from https://www.psychologytoday.com/us/blog/high-octane-women/201205/where-do-you-fall-the-burnout-continuum

Chartock, J., & Wiener, R. (2014). How to save teachers from burning out, dropping out and other hazards of experience. The Hechinger Report.

Coda, R., & Jetter, R. (2016). *Escaping the School Leader's Dunk Tank: How to prevail when others want to see you drown*. San Diego, CA: Dave Burgess Consulting.

Couros, G. (2015). *The Innovator's Mindset: Empower learning, unleash talent, and lead a culture of creativity*. San Diego, CA: Dave Burgess Consulting.

Crowe, C. (Director). (1996). Jerry Maguire [Motion picture]. Burbank, California: TriStar Pictures.

REFERENCES

Dictionary by Merriam-Webster: America's most-trusted online dictionary. (n.d.). Retrieved September 29, 2018, from https://www.merriam-webster.com/

Dweck, C. (n.d.). Mindset: What is it? Retrieved August 25, 2018, from https://mindsetonline.com/whatisit/about/index.html

Economy, P. (2014, October 17). 10 Powerful Habits of Highly Effective Leaders. Retrieved August 25, 2018, from https://www.inc.com/peter-economy/10-powerful-habits-of-highly-effective-leaders.html

Froehlich, M. (2018). *The Fire Within: Lessons from defeat that have ignited a passion for learning.* Alexandria, VA: EduMatch.

Grant Rankin, J., Ph.D. (2016). The Teacher Burnout Epidemic: How prevalent is burnout in the teaching profession? Retrieved August 25, 2018, from https://www.psychologytoday.com/us/blog/much-more-common-core/201611/the-teacher-burnout-epidemic-part-1-2

Gruenert, S. (2008, March). School Culture, School Climate: They are not the same thing. *NAESP.* Retrieved August 25, 2018, from https://www.naesp.org/sites/default/files/resources/2/Principal/2008/M-Ap56.pdf

Heath, C., & Heath, D. (2017). *The power of moments: Why certain experiences have extraordinary impact.* London: Bantam Press.

Ingersoll, R. M. (2012). Beginning teacher induction what the data tell us. Phi Delta Kappan, 93(8), 47-51.

Ingersoll, R., Merrill, L., & Stuckey, D. (2014). Seven trends: The transformation of the teaching force.

James, G. (2012, July 30). How to Conquer Fear: 4 Mental Tricks. Retrieved October 25, 2018, from https://www.inc.com/geoffrey-james/how-to-conquer-fear-4-mental-tricks.html

Mark, J. J. (2010, July 14). Heraclitus of Ephesus. Retrieved August 24, 2018, from https://www.ancient.eu/Heraclitus_of_Ephesos/

Michael Jr. (2017, January 08). Retrieved August 26, 2018, from https://youtu.be/1ytFB8TrkTo

Murphy, M. (2018, April 15). *Neuroscience Explains Why You Need to Write Down Your Goals If You Actually Want to Achieve Them*. Forbes. Retrieved September 2, 2018, from https://www.forbes.com/sites/markmurphy/2018/04/15/neuroscience-explains-why-you-need-to-write-down-your-goals-if-you-actually-want-to-achieve-them/#5f12047e7905

Neufeld, S. (2014). Can a teacher be too dedicated? The Atlantic.

Rigsby, R. (2017, December 15). The Wisdom of a Third Grade Dropout (Goalcast, Ed.). Retrieved August 25, 2018, from https://www.goalcast.com/2017/10/06/rick-rigsby-the-wisdom-of-a-third-grade-dropout/

Routman, R. (2014). *Read, write, lead: Breakthrough strategies for schoolwide literacy success.* Alexandria, VA: ASCD.

Secondary Traumatic Stress. (n.d.). Retrieved August 25, 2018, from https://www.acf.hhs.gov/trauma-toolkit/secondary-traumatic-stress

Seidel, A. (2014, July 18). The teacher dropout crisis. Retrieved from https://www.npr.org/sections/ed/2014/07/18/332343240/the-teacher-dropout-crisis

Sinek, S. (n.d.). Start with Why. Retrieved September 5, 2018, from https://startwithwhy.com/

Spencer, J., & Juliani, A. J. (2016). Launch: Using design thinking to boost creativity and bring out the maker in every student. Dave Burgess Consulting, Incorporated.

Wettrick, D. (2017). *Pure Genius.* San Diego, CA: Dave Burgess Consulting.

Wong, H. K., & Wong, R. T. (1991). *The first days of school.* Sunnyvale, CA: Harry K. Wong Publications.

Mandy Froehlich is a Director of Innovation and Technology, national speaker, and author from Wisconsin where she supports and encourages educators to create innovative change in their classrooms. Her passion lies in reinvigorating and re-engaging teachers back into their profession, as well as advocating for what is needed to support teachers in their pursuit of innovative and divergent thinking. She consults with school districts and post-secondary institutions around the country on the effective use of technology to support great teaching, as a Google for Education Certified Trainer and has presented on similar topics at conferences such as CUE, TIES, FETC and ISTE. Her first book, *The Fire Within: Lessons from defeat that have ignited a passion for learning*, discusses mental health awareness for teachers.

Also by Mandy Froehlich

Adversity itself is not what defines us. It is how we react to that adversity and the choices we make that creates who we are and how we will persevere. The Fire Within: Lessons from defeat that have ignited a passion for learning is a compilation of stories from amazing educators who have faced personal adversity head on and have become stronger people for it.

Other EduMatch Titles

This book started as a series of separate writing pieces that were eventually woven together to form a fabric called The Y in You. The question is, "What's the 'why' in you?" Why do you? Why would you? Why should you? Through the pages in this book, you will gain the confidence to be you, and understand the very power in what being you can produce.

Follow the Teacher's Journey with Brian as he weaves together the stories of seven incredible educators. Each step encourages educators at any level to reflect, grow, and connect. The Teacher's Journey will ignite your mind and heart through its practical ideas and vulnerable storytelling.

This book challenges the thought that "teaching" begins only after certification and college graduation. Instead, it describes how students in teacher preparation programs have value to offer their future colleagues, even as they are learning to be teachers!

Made in the USA
Columbia, SC
11 August 2019